DATE DUE			
MAY 1 2 1988			
OCT 02 2018			

How Philosophy Uses Its Past

How Philosophy
Uses Its Past

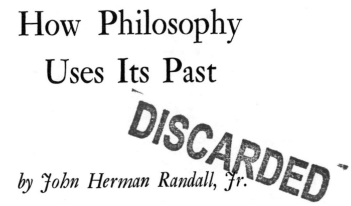

by John Herman Randall, Jr.

GREENWOOD PRESS, PUBLISHERS
WESTPORT, CONNECTICUT

Library of Congress Cataloging in Publication Data

Randall, John Hermann, 1899-
  How philosophy uses its past.

    Reprint. Originally published: New York : Columbia
University Press, 1963. (Matchette lectures ; 14)
    Includes index.
    1. Philosophy--History--Study and teaching--
Addresses, essays, lectures. I. Title.
[B52.R25 1983]   109   83-12754
ISBN 0-313-24127-9 (lib. bdg.)

Reprinted in 1983 by Greenwood Press
A division of Congressional Information Service, Inc.
88 Post Road West, Westport, Connecticut 06881

Printed in the United States of America

10 9 8 7 6 5 4 3 2 1

To my Friend

Albert Gordon Redpath

Contents

Foreword

These Matchette Lectures presented by Professor Randall at Wesleyan University in the spring of 1961 were the fourteenth in the series of lectures which were initiated by the late Irwin Edman. It is a pleasure to express here, perhaps publicly in print for the first time, Wesleyan's sincere gratitude to the Franklin J. Matchette Foundation for making possible this important series of lectures in which some of the most distinguished American philosophers like William E. Hocking, C. I. Lewis, Susanne Langer, Brand Blanshard, and Paul Tillich have appeared. Professor Randall's admirable lectures on the contribution of history to philosophical understanding gave heartening and impressive support to the policy of the Department of Philosophy, initiated in 1888 by the late Professor Andrew C. Armstrong, and continued ever since, to stress the paramount value of the history of philosophy for an understanding of philosophy and the attainment of proficiency in it. The maintenance of such a policy during more than seventy-five years was not easy in view of modern temptations to relegate the history of philosophy to a secondary position in favor of courses representing the latest trends in contemporary philosophy.

The central problem in such an emphasis on the historical approach to philosophy is how great interest in the past can be combined with sensitivity to modern needs. Only a person perfectly at home in both realms of philosophy, its past and its present, could hope effectively to exhibit the relevance of philosophy's past to modern concerns and preoccupations. This Professor Randall is well qualified to do. He is a distinguished American scholar in the field of the history of philosophy. He himself relates that it was Dean Frederick J. E. Woodbridge at Columbia who first stirred his philosophical and historical imagination and, interestingly, it is of Dean Woodbridge that Sterling Lamprecht wrote: "He was a leader, possibly *the* leader in the movement in the United States in the twentieth century which made the history of philosophy one of the major philosophical disciplines." Following Professor Randall's publishing of *The Making of the Modern Mind*, in 1926, now a universally known classic in the field of the history of Western culture, he has steadily produced, though by no means restricting himself to the history of philosophy, a whole series of historical works at once recognized for their distinction in scholarship and their fresh interpretations and new insights based on new historical discoveries. The appearance of his *Aristotle*, in 1960, and the first volume of his monumental work, *The Career of Philosophy*, in 1962, have been hailed with delight by students and acclaimed by colleagues everywhere for their high distinction in scholarship and their comprehensiveness of scope.

In these Matchette Lectures Professor Randall addresses himself to the objection often raised by contemporary philosophers that if the history of philosophy were to be regarded as the essence of philosophy it could have no further history. It will be remembered that the New Realists of 1912 and the Critical Realists of 1920 made similar observations in their cooperative volumes and expressed the hope that their cooperative efforts would help philosophy approach the much envied success of the sciences by isolation of a given problem and cooperative attack upon it. Their lack of success in subsequent cooperation served to justify William James's characterization of the philosopher as a "lone beast dwelling in his individual burrow," not well endowed for cooperative enterprises.

In the first place, in these lectures Professor Randall fully agrees that philosophy is much more than its history, but he also insists that without knowledge of its history and the utilization of its rich resources, philosophizing is bound to be rather "thin and ultimately empty." Furthermore, while James may be right that at any given time philosophers may indeed not seem to be distinguished for success in cooperative enterprises, the whole history of philosophy, Professor Randall demonstrates, over and over again displays the development of a given cluster of ideas through the perhaps unpremeditated but nevertheless most effective cooperation of successive generations of thinkers who, to begin with, adopt a certain general point of view like continental rationalism or British empiricism, but aided by detachment from some of the too intense special concerns of their predecessors proceed to work out with fresh insight and open mindedness both the implicit advantages and the shortcomings of the initial position.

It would, then, seem that for man "writ large," in time as well as in space, the history of philosophy operates like the individual's memory which Plato always emphasized as one of the prime prerequisites for a philosopher. In philosophy as elsewhere there is no substitute for experience, and the history of philosophy with its rich heritage provides contemporary philosophers with valuable experience that can safeguard them from entering upon philosophical impasses and can offer them the necessary tools for dealing with important modern issues, like those of individualism and human freedom, the role of intelligence and the appraisal of values in human affairs, and the relevance of stoic "natural law" to our present international situation.

In his recurrent discussion of the problem of the nature of philosophy, persistently in dispute in recent contemporary philosophy, Professor Randall makes clear his own position: there *is* a *philosophia perennis*, not telling as Hegel believed only *one* story but many stories, which are nevertheless interconnected, and there are persistent and perennial problems in philosophy in spite of a great variety of language and diversity of approaches. Readers of Professor Randall's previous historical books will recall his judgment that Plato and Aristotle are never so alive as today and continue to be a challenge to fresh interpretation. Professor Randall refers approvingly to Bertrand Russell's recent statement that "all Western philosophy is Greek philosophy." But not only the Greeks, but Spinoza and Kant, and, in fact, all the great leaders of philosophical thought of the past, are our intellectual contemporaries whom we ignore or neglect at our peril.

Professor Randall is also, it would appear, in harmony with John Dewey's celebrated judgment that "philosophy recovers itself when it ceases to be a device for dealing with the problems of philosophers and becomes a method, cultivated by philosophers, for dealing with the problems of men." Professor Randall concludes that throughout its long history philosophy has revealed itself to be "a clarification and criticism of fundamental beliefs involved in all the great enterprises of human culture, science, art, religion, the moral life, social and political activity." In addition, the study of philosophy's history also illumines its imaginative and poetic

function, which has been enormously fruitful in many areas
of man's intellectual life. The classic visions of philosophy
afford imaginative liberation of the mind and free men from
provincialism, insularity, and narrowness of point of view.
The great philosophers are the intellectual statesmen of the
day.

One of the most interesting suggestions in these lectures is
that on the basis of the examination of the successive critical
developments of rival historical patterns of approach there
seems to be discernible a recurrent tendency toward an
eventual convergence of various traditions toward a common
metaphysics. Professor Randall expresses the belief and hope
that different philosophical languages expressive of different
philosophical traditions may once more be "approaching the
point where they are ultimately translatable into each other's
terms—perhaps in the end into a common tongue." It is
precisely the history of philosophy that can serve as an effective interpreter in facilitating this advance toward a mutual
understanding.

The abundance of illustrative material, ranging over the
whole course of the history of Western philosophy, presented
in support of the analyses of these lectures makes for fascinating and instructive reading for students and colleagues alike.
The style of exposition, as the reader will soon discover, is
distinguished throughout by Professor Randall's clarity of
statement, enlivened by his characteristic wit. Particularly
delightful is his imaginative delineation, in the first chapter of
the book, of the vicissitudes, the ups and downs, the "gran-
deur" and "misère" of Lady Philosophy in her long career
as alternately the queenly mistress and the humble servant
in and out of her household. It is especially to be

hoped that students who initially only wish to hear and read about "le dernier cri" in philosophy will be charmed and persuaded by these lectures to undertake on their own a serious study of the story of philosophy.

CORNELIUS KRUSÉ

Wesleyan University
Middletown, Connecticut

I. The Cultural
Functions of Philosophy

It is customary to begin any discussion of philosophy by
defining philosophy itself. But the student of philosophy as a
reasonably systematic and responsible discipline, especially if
he is a professional and claims the right of economic support
for what he so obviously enjoys doing, and would go on doing
whether paid to do it or not, compared with most of his colleagues is at some disadvantage. To explain to them just what
he is engaged upon, just what his "field" is, is not easy. We
have all of us a general notion of what the mathematician is
about, or even the economist. To be sure, to define just what
mathematics is has come to be one of the most difficult tasks
of the mathematician. In our day it has even been seriously
questioned whether mathematics is a "science" or not—mathematics, from which the Greeks, who invented both it and
science, derived their very conception of what constitutes a
science! Perhaps the most interesting definition is that given
by a great mathematician, Bertrand Russell: "Mathematics is
the science in which we do not know what we are talking
about, or whether what we are saying is true or not."

It might be objected that this is not a very satisfactory
definition, for it hardly serves to distinguish mathematics from
philosophy. But then, Russell is not only a mathematician, he
is a mathematical philosopher; and what he is really defining
is the philosopher's understanding of mathematics. But it

would be as well not to follow up this theme at the moment. It would also be well not to try to list some other academically respectable disciplines whose practitioners are also often embarrassed when asked to make clear their serious intentions toward knowledge. There is psychology, for instance, and that old whipping-boy, sociology.

In those casual encounters, formerly in Pullman smoking compartments, and more recently in jet planes, in which a stranger innocently asks what I do to justify my support by society, I fear I have fallen into a cowardly habit. I have myself retreated to the safe answer, "I am an historian." This, I find, usually satisfies him. I do not go on to tell him I have given a number of courses, and written at least one book, to try to find an answer to the question I have found equally perplexing, "What is history?" He might then, if he were reasonably astute, begin to suspect that I was masquerading under false pretenses, and that I am really a philosopher.

But am I really a philosopher? When, as a student of philosophy, I ask myself that perplexing question, the best evidence I can find for the affirmative answer I should like to give, is that I do find so many such questions so perplexing. The philosopher is the man who, with some intellectual pretensions, and not the mere indifference of the ordinary citizen, finds most of the things men do and say and ask are apt to set him wondering. Philosophy, remarked Aristotle, who ought to know, for there would be general agreement he at least is a philosopher, philosophy begins in wonder. He thought it could not begin until, like the Egyptian priests, who were to the Greeks what the Greeks are to us, the symbols of ancient wisdom, one had had enough to eat. But some of the most important philosophies have begun when the comfortably fed, like the Buddha, or like Karl Marx, observed that most men did not have enough to eat. What do philosophers wonder about, that makes them not mere idle daydreamers, like most children, but philosophers, a distinctive breed? Sometimes they wonder about the world in which they find themselves, the natural and the human and the social world. They just wonder and ask questions. Sometimes they wonder about more particular questions, like why men do not have enough to eat, and what we can do about it for them; or like why there are sociologists.

Philosophers sometimes wonder about definite things, and sometimes they just wonder. They are perplexed that things should be as they are. At times they are perplexed that things should be; at times they are just perplexed. My teacher, who was the wisest philosopher I have ever known personally, had a favorite and characteristic saying. He would remark, "I am perplexed. I wonder—." He once got into trouble by saying in a talk in Berlin, "Ich bewundere mich." In his case that remark was wholly innocent, springing, as Dr. Johnson said on a similar occasion, from pure ignorance—of the German tongue. But other philosophers have come to hold that attitude consciously. They have not only wondered, they have also found the answer. Now finding the answer is also philosophy, of a sort. Indeed today, to say nothing of the past, it is quite usual to find professional philosophers convinced that they have found out and are in possession of all the answers. And the questions to which they do not know the answers are not worth asking. Only scientists ask that kind of questions, and scholars, not philosophers, who are more sophisticated. The philosopher is the man who knows the right kind of questions to ask, the answerable kind, to whose solution he holds the key. He will patiently explain to you why yours are foolish to ask, for they can never receive an answer.

This suggests another feature that is also characteristic of philosophers. Even those philosophers who have not professed, like the usual run-of-the-mill variety, to know all the answers, have usually been convinced the other fellow's answers are all wrong. Socrates, for instance, was good at wondering, and his professional badge was his claim that he had not yet found the answers. But he went about Athens buttonholing other men, enticing them into a conversation in which he would triumphantly prove that they did not know the answers either, and were indeed far worse off than himself, for they did not even know they did not know the answers.

Socrates has ever since been the very symbol of philosophy, the patron saint of all subsequent philosophers. But few of them have ever professed his own Socratic ignorance. For we know about Socrates from the pictures Plato has given of him philosophizing, that is, using all the tricks of the trade of a generation of sophisticated sophists, to browbeat his victims into an ultimate confession of their pretentious ignorance. Socrates must have been something like that, for whatever he did, it made him so popular he was put to death, in what Plato made one of the most famous deaths of all history. That, among other reasons, is why I usually tell casual strangers I am an historian, and conceal the truth. When I do not want to be disturbed by further conversation, I sometimes venture to answer, I teach philosophy. The result is always predictable. The stranger says, "Oh!—I wonder how much longer that man in the White House is going to spend our hard-earned money," and soon starts talking to someone else.

But Socrates, though a wonderful teacher, did not succeed in teaching his successors his ignorance. For they read about him in the pages of Plato. And Plato, though he was clearly fascinated by Socrates, did not agree with him. Plato found the answers; and the successors have in that respect followed him and not his teacher. But Plato had learned enough from Socrates to put the answers in such a form that nobody since has been quite able to be sure what they are. And they have been arguing about it ever since. They have some of them been pretty good philosophers, from Aristotle down. For if philosophy begins in wonder, and ought, as Socrates counseled, to confess an ignorance about the answers, it at any rate always ends in arguing. Even Socrates, as Plato depicts him, ended by arguing; and he is shown arguing so hard and to such purpose that he usually forgets he does not know the answers and goes on arguing for them—Plato's answers. Wonder and argument are the function of philosophy—and, the unregenerate have always liked to add, ignorance in the end.

Kant was another great philosopher who claimed not to know the answers to the questions men asked and to which they wanted a solution. And he too was pretty hard on those who claimed they had them all, the confident dogmatists of the Age of Reason. But in his day the world was more civilized, and did not put Kant to death. Instead, they took him as showing that since men could not find by argument and reason the answers they knew were so, they were entitled to believe them anyway. From that license Kant was supposed to have issued has descended one of the most popular philosophies of the present day, existentialism. It knows how to arrive at the answers without arguing about them; it believes in the will to believe. But then even it has to argue for the right to get the solution without argument.

Existentialism has a positive message to preach to us today. But another popular philosophy—more popular among academic intellectuals, in fact—has a different kind of message, more negative, and hence more appealing to the academic profession. It tells us that the answers other philosophers have given us are all wrong, because they asked the wrong kind of questions. The function of philosophy is to get us to stop asking those questions, so we can go on talking without being perplexed. If that be indeed the function of philosophy, a great future can be predicted for it. For there will always be enough perplexed souls to demand the therapeutic treatment.

Why are they perplexed? Speaking from my own experience, I can only say, they seem to be made that way. Whether they are born that way, or rather made that way by being miseducated, as I was miseducated, first by my father and then by my teacher, is not too clear. But if it is the fault of education and not of nature, that makes no real difference. The materials of our education have themselves been made such that we can now educate no one without giving him a certain strain of philosophical perplexity. And being human and modern, we all have to be educated—though even that is something I am occasionally led to wonder about. Fortunately we have arranged our society so that the wonder and the perplexity, and even the arguing, are soon enough repressed when we start making a living. But not in everybody. And there are enough of us who go on wondering, and enough who, though they have pretty well learned the lesson of present-day philosophy, and stopped wondering, still remember the former delight they enjoyed when younger, to appoint certain people to wonder and be perplexed professionally. Even if these professionals should all decide their chief job was to cure the bad habit of wondering, somebody else would be sure to crop up and start it all over again. One thing I do not wonder about is whether all men will not eventually stop wondering. The answer to that one I think I know.

Most philosophers have managed to come up with the answers. The difficulty that has always been felt about their conclusions has been that there were so many of them, and they were so different. But in the past there was usually some agreement about the questions. What the philosopher was supposed to think about got settled fairly early in what we call the classic tradition. In the generation after Aristotle, the Epicureans and especially the Stoics made it clear that they were to think about the world, and about human life, and about the proper way to argue about both. Philosophy was to be made up of logic, the study of thinking and arguing; physics, the study about the world and its relation to the gods or God; and ethics, the study of the chief good of man. But in recent days those traditional fields of philosophical thought and argument have been seriously questioned. Logic has stood up pretty well, and is still going more strongly than ever. But it has become a branch of mathematics, and as such it interests only a minority of mathematicians themselves. A generation ago it was the world that attracted considerable philosophical attention. The physicists were just telling us the extraordinary things they had been discovering about it, and that excited philosophical wonder and the demand for clarification. But what they said got so complicated that it took physicists and the other scientists to wonder to much purpose about it. The professional philosophers were not prepared to be perplexed to any purpose about its newly discovered features in particular; only Whitehead the physicist was up to the challenge. The rest were merely perplexed, and they decided to leave the world to the scientists, since few of them were. Russell took to saying that if he had to do it all over again, he would be a physicist: that could excite his ineradicable philosophical impulse to wonder in the light of new knowledge.

As for ethics, thinking about human life and the good of

man, the existentialists have been telling us to make what we want out of it, and the Oxford philosophers have been concerned with the way we talk about it. What to do about it, they say, is not the task of the philosopher, but of the moralist and the preacher, who probably do not know anyway. And as for the other traditional questions, our wonder has led us only into dilemmas. Since we cannot wonder without talking, at least teachers and other corrupters of the young cannot, we should concentrate on the study of talking, in the hope we can learn to talk less confusedly, which is all to the good.

And so we seem to be back with Aristotle again. He always begins his inquiries with the way we talk about questions, and where his predecessors have talked the wrong way. Perhaps we are even ready to go on, as Aristotle himself always goes on, to look at the world we want to talk about, when we have got straightened out on the best way to talk. Aristotle goes so far as to hold that we can talk best about things if we have found something out about them. Cambridge has always held that, though usually it has insisted we do not need to find out much; but we certainly ought to know mathematics. But Oxford seems hardly prepared to accept that Aristotelian heresy. It has not yet forgotten the enormous amount of talking the last two generations did there, most of which it judges to have been pretty foolish. Let us hope that when Oxford has learned how to talk, even if it is only ordinary English, it will go on to say something. For when it has got started, in the past Oxford has usually had a good deal to say.

We set out to indicate some of the reasons why it is not too easy to define philosophy, or even to make at all clear to one who does not already know, what is its "field." Indeed, it has often been objected, by scientists on the one hand and poets on the other, especially of late, when our academic disciplines have become so compartmentalized, that philosophy has no "field" of its own. The objection has some justice. Or rather, the "field" of philosophy is a domain as broad as human life itself. For in this wide world of ours, there is nothing that cannot on occasion, and few things that have not, been able to excite the philosopher's wonder, nothing at which he cannot be, and in point of fact has not been, perplexed. But is it any easier to delimit the field of the poet? Is there anything to which, if in him feeling and thought be fused, he cannot give poetic expression? Or can we set bounds to science? Is there anything in human experience the mind of man cannot seek to know about, by means of controlled and critical and responsible intellectual methods? And how about religion, which has always proudly claimed to embrace the whole of life, and which no man has ever been able to define to the satisfaction of many others?

No, these great human enterprises are not easily definable: every definition turns out to be the expression of a particular and limited perspective. And of philosophy this has always been true, since the days of the Greeks, who invented the whole enterprise. But today we encounter a still more perplexing difficulty. Philosophers have always failed to agree about their conclusions, between schools and even between individuals. For the schools have been organized about distinctive interests and insights, about those perspectives on life which can indeed be shared, but not exclusively, or universally. And there inevitably remains something of the personal and the unique about every really great philosopher, which has certainly not lessened since the Romanticists set originality above soundness, and individuality above impersonal objectivity. Philosophers have always differed in their conclusions, and, as we shall see, over the generations they have differed in the questions they have asked. But in the West, at any one time at least, they have usually had the sense of belonging to a common enterprise. Today that is hardly any longer true. At present philosophical schools seem more deeply divided than they have ever been before. For they have come to differ on the very conception they entertain of the nature of the philosophic enterprise. There is no agreement among them as to the function of philosophizing itself.

Why this is so today, and how this situation developed, is a question we shall have to return to later. This is one of the facts about philosophy that cries for the illumination that historical knowledge and analysis can alone give. And we shall find, I think, that in the perspectives of its history, our present sharp disagreement on the very function of philosophy is not quite so ultimate as in our polemical or our nostalgic moments we often imagine. But the fact remains, that to attempt at the outset to define the nature and function of philosophy in terms of any one of the programs of the major groups today, would at once involve us in taking sides with a particular perspective. In the end we can hardly avoid a taking sides, at least in the sense of rejecting some of the exclusive and negative claims so loudly announced in our day. But that commitment can hardly come as a responsible and informed decision, until we have explored the historical dimension of philosophizing.

Even here, we may appear to be rejecting a tenet of several of our contemporary philosophical gospels. For there is abroad the conviction that whatever philosophizing has been in the past, it must henceforth be different. We would do well to disregard that past, which for us has receded into the limbo of mere history. The knowledge of the past functioning of the philosophic enterprise may indeed be fascinating, as for many it clearly is. But the history of philosophy is not philosophizing itself. And as responsible philosophers, when we are about our serious pursuit, we have the obligation to put it resolutely behind us.

There are indeed clear reasons why present-day philosophical movements have felt it necessary to turn their backs on history. They are reasons which it requires the light of recent history itself to illuminate. In part, it is a central element in the intellectual temper of our age—in what we used to call the *Zeitgeist*, but that is itself an historical concept we should do well for the moment not to employ—to have turned away with a certain scorn from what is called nineteenth-century "historicism." Just what "historicism" may be, or have been, is none too clear; I am afraid that too demands some historical analysis for its clarification. To be sure, there never was a time when men had such an interest in history, and when historical accounts of new knowledge about portions of the past that have hitherto remained obscure, and historical reinterpretations of what we had thought we had been long familiar with, have found a more ready and eager welcome in the intellectual community. But it remains a fact that we have come to compartmentalize history, as so much else, and to set it off rather sharply from the theoretical analysis to which we have now once more turned in hopeful anticipation.

That very compartmentalization is another controlling reason for the separation of the analytic from the historical dimension of philosophy. Like all our other intellectual pursuits, philosophy has felt the urge to immerse itself in what Russell calls our "fierce specialisms." In our century new techniques and procedures have been developed, and they are so fascinating in themselves, and promise so much in the way of further advance, that it is little wonder those attracted by them have small time or energy for a broader view. Symbolic logic, linguistic analysis, phenomenological research —the immediate future seems clearly to belong to their exploration.

This is coupled with the urge to make philosophy itself a distinctive discipline, with a clearly demarcated field of its own, and procedures that set it off from other disciplines. Like everything else, philosophy must of course today be, if not "scientific," at least *wissenschaftlich*. But the mother of sciences must not live in the household of her children: she must preserve a home of her own. Philosophy must be a separate family unit; there must be no doubt it is different from both science and history. A few years ago a distinguished representative of one of the modern specialisms, himself the possessor of wide historical scholarship, told us that practitioners of philosophy are quite different from those who enter a laboratory—that is science; nor do they spend time in the library— that is historical scholarship. I have heard another, in what I trust was an unguarded moment, remark that a philosopher ought not to know too much about science or history; it would be apt to spoil his thinking as a philosopher. Can it be that the heirs of the proud confidence and assurance of Hegel are now suffering from an inferiority complex?

There are thus distinctive reasons today why the more evangelical philosophical movements should feel the urge to separate their promising programs from historical study. But at bottom, has not this always been the case? A new philosophical impulse has always been so concerned with the future that it has usually not wasted much time on the past. It has often, indeed, perhaps, usually, fancied it was turning its back on the "schools" completely, and making a wholly fresh start.

Descartes saw himself in just that light—though today we realize he was mistaken—and Bacon. To our minds, Kant had a curious lack of interest in history, even in the achievements of the Greeks he was trying to reclaim. The great pioneers of the seventeenth century are in their *tours de force* so stimulating still, in part at least, just because, with the exception of Leibniz, of their sublime disregard for the past, and because they do not feel they are working in an historical museum. One wonders what Descartes would have accomplished had he studied Gilson carefully, or how Spinoza would have expressed his vision had he been thoroughly familiar with Wolfson. And the great critics of the eighteenth century, Berkeley and Hume and Kant and the rest, seem supremely indifferent to the historical reasons for the outgrown assumptions and prejudices that, in the endeavor to bring men's thinking up-to-date, they are pruning away.

The periods when philosophy did become institutionalized, and preserved in its "schools" something of the continuity and cumulative advance we associate with the sciences, seem on the whole to have achieved more continuity than advance. The Hellenistic schools, even that of Aristotle, unless we conceive his endeavors to have shifted to Alexandria and Rhodes, strike us as a slow petering out. Ever since the seventeenth century the medieval schools have served as a byword for mere traditionalism. And more recently, the Hegelian school never rose, even in a Bradley, to the heights of its founder. After all, turning one's back on the past has pretty good philosophical precedent, and very plausible arguments in its support.

We may still ask, however, can it be done without irreparable loss? That is the question we are here trying to explore. Can we really disregard the historical dimensions of philosophy, even when our primary concern is with its analytic or even—God save the mark!—its speculative or "synoptic" dimensions? And we have already at the outset raised a question which it seems impossible to answer without turning to that historical dimension. What is philosophy? What is the function of philosophizing? What is the nature of the philosophical enterprise itself? We have seen how we can hardly answer that question in purely contemporary terms without a premature taking of sides. In the end we must come out with a conception that will give direction to what we ourselves judge ultimately most worth doing. But can we make a responsible and informed decision, without knowing at least what philosophy has been, and what in our long tradition has been the function philosophizing has served? Like all historical knowledge, to be sure, an acquaintance and familiarity with what ends philosophizing has served in the past will not of itself determine for us our decision as to what goal to bend it to in our own day. But it will illuminate our decision. Historical knowledge is not in itself an evaluation, and the conviction that it is sufficient is a fallacy from which our present schools have wisely sought liberation. But at the same time it is a necessary condition of any responsible and properly critical judgment of value.

It is only fair to serve warning that I myself do possess a definite conception of the nature and function of philosophic thinking. That conception has grown out of an examination of the philosophers themselves, of the problems and ideas that have seemed to them important. It has taken form for me as those problems and ideas, when pressed, revealed why they both seemed and were actually important, why they drove acute and imaginative minds to searching thought, to subtle criticism and poetic vision. It has led me to the climate of opinion out of which past structures of ideas arose, to the great social and intellectual conflicts that drove men to construct them; it has revealed to me those structures performing in the world of men that function for which they were created.

So it seems idle to try to analyze philosophy's character in ignorance of her useful deeds. It is far wiser to approach her when we are acquainted with the story of her life. I have tried to piece it together carefully from the memoirs she has left. She belongs to the oldest profession in the world: she exists to give men pleasure, and to satisfy their imperious needs. When young and blooming, she was a favorite of the rich but cultivated and discriminating Greeks, who kept her in idleness for the sheer delight of her conversation. She did not even have to lift a finger, save to help with geometry; and it was rumored the gods loved her, and, Aristotle reports, her alone. But as she grew older, her charms began to fade, she waxed more austere, and took to giving sound moral advice on every occasion. And when the Romans burst into her garden, with their American moralism and their fear of idleness, they led her off and set her to work as the handmaiden of morality, carrying the Romans' burden. She has been a working-girl ever since. Most of her life she spent in serving her mistress Theology; but she began to wax independent, and took to putting the old lady in her place. From this servitude she was rescued by a handsome young admirer, who loved to hear the tales of her ancient glory in her earlier days with the Greeks. But she was soon enslaved again by Science, who set her to work clearing fields and putting up fences. Again and again Science found her invaluable in private, but grew apt to cut her dead in public.

She has just put in a century working for the faith of our grandmothers. But the old lady passed on at last, bequeathing her effects to the brazen young Neo-orthodoxy, who will have nothing to do with her. At present she still has a pension from the rich but ailing old Capitalism, but she has been engaged for part-time work by the up-and-coming heirs of Marx and Lenin. In the meantime, she keeps busy cleaning up for the physicists, and has just got a job revising the Oxford dictionary. For all the hard work she has done, she is scarcely an honest woman; and notoriously, though the Americans tried to entice her into the kitchen, she can really bake no bread. For centuries she has enjoyed most being a camp follower: you will find her always where the fighting has been fiercest, wherever men have been torn loose from their family and domestic ties, and want to fraternize, when their wives have been left behind, or have run away, or have just grown too wrinkled and old. She consorts with the fighters, comforts them, tells them what they want to hear; and with the wisdom of her incredible experience, counsels them how to win. No wonder countless soldiers in the strife of ideas have thought her the one woman in the world, *das Ewig-Weibliche,* and have sworn to her undying allegiance. But *mutabilis semper femina.* She turns up in some other camp with a new set of finery. She is indispensable, but quite without conscience. She serves any man with the desire to know.

The story of philosophy's life illuminates her character. She has always been the handmaiden and the camp follower of men's ideas and ideals. For long periods she has performed faithful but menial service. Then she suddenly breaks loose and appears with the fighters, for new and old alike. She labors to set their baggage and their weapons in order, trying to organize them into some tidier and reasonably manageable arrangement, fitting opposed or irrelevant beliefs together into some not too chaotic scheme, adjusting warring values to give some fairly unified direction to life, without excluding too much; forging new weapons out of the shattered remnants of the old; always leading men on to fresh terrain and newly won elevations, to the unexpected consequences of their ideas. And she pauses, now and again, to point to tantalizing glimpses of something calm and serene above the tumult.

The main features of human experience remain universal: birth, growing up, making a living, getting on with one's fellows—the urge of sex, the piercing ecstasy of love, the desire to understand—failure, frustration, bereavement, sickness, and death. And this universal pattern of living finds some expression in all those really comprehensive philosophies, which, starting as battle cries in some human struggle, have yet managed to raise themselves above the conflict to a broader perspective on man's life in the world. But the particular ways in which these universal experiences are met and ritualized, above all the particular beliefs in terms of which they have been articulated and rationalized, present a bewildering variety. Especially is this true of those conflicts between ideas which lead to the searching thinking that becomes philosophy, that fresh impingement of novel social experience upon traditional beliefs and values which drives men to construct their systems and structures of thought, the confrontation with new ideas irrelevant to, or even totally incompatible with the old and familiar, which yet have somehow to be adjusted to them and worked into the accustomed pattern of men's thinking and living. Especially are these cultural conflicts in each case historically unique.

Philosophic problems can only be defined operationally, as those questions in which philosophic minds have become interested. Or, what amounts to the same thing, they are those problems which have succeeded in generating a philosophic response, and have given birth to philosophers and philosophical questions and answers. They emerge, the record reveals, whenever the strife of ideas and experiences forces men back to the fundamental assumptions in any field; when it compels men to analyze them, to clarify, criticize, and reconstruct them. If this be the case—and one cannot explore the historical dimensions of philosophizing without having the conviction forced on one that it is so—then the problems that initiate philosophizing have varied from age to age. They are to be understood ultimately only as expressions of the basic conflicts within a culture that drive men to thoroughgoing analysis and criticism.

Philosophizing can be also a purely individual enterprise: it can serve the function of a rational—or a rationalized—substitute for a religious faith grown no longer possible. It can be primarily a way of deliverance for the troubled in spirit, as it was for the ancient Hellenistic schools, for the Stoic or the Epicurean or the Sceptic, and probably for the less intellectual of the Platonists. Or it can be a hardwon personal perspective upon the world, an individual *Weltanschauung*, worked out by a man from his own private standpoint, giving him, and perhaps him alone, the way to understand the wealth and chaotic diversity of experience in intellectually manageable form. For a Spinoza it was both; but for him, though it led him to articulate an impersonal vision, the personal function was doubtless controlling. The vision is quite different, but the combination of a way of understanding and a way of deliverance, with a strongly personal accent, is the same in Lucretius.

But the historical record points not only to philosophy as a personal way of understanding and of finding salvation. It points also to philosophizing as having possessed, from its first beginnings with the Milesians, a social and cultural function as well. Philosophy has been, and ultimately remains, a social enterprise, as well as—indeed, men being the social creatures they are, before it can become—a private and personal way of accepting the universe and coming to terms with the conditions of human life. And as a social and cultural enterprise, philosophizing is the expression in thinking of cultural change itself. In the Hegelian language, at once suggestive and in need of careful qualification, philosophy is the intellectual phase or moment of the process by which cultural conflicts, or social conflicts of cultural significance, are analyzed and clarified, sometimes resolved and composed, more often transformed into further intellectual problems, so that the life of man thinking may proceed. Philosophy is the criticism of the fundamental beliefs in any of man's great cultural enterprises, science, art, religion, the moral life, social and practical activity, when some new idea or some altered experience has impinged upon them and generated intellectual tensions and maladjustments.

This distinctive cultural and historical function of philosophical thinking is the reason why Western civilization, with its never-ending succession of intellectual tensions and conflicts, has exhibited so rich a record of philosophical achievement. It is the reason why our present task of organizing our world-wide industrial and scientific culture, so sorely calls for philosophical analysis and reflection today, and offers so golden an opportunity for fresh philosophical accomplishment. I do not mind being pessimistic on occasion. But I am convinced, for any man with a genuine philosophic impulse this is a glorious age in which to be alive—if we can only manage to stay that way. But the exhilaration of danger only makes the opportuinty all the more challenging. A civilization that has grown stable and static may have inherited what we sometimes call "a philosophy." But it produces no philosophic thinking. That comes only with tensions and conflicts and problems.

The specific problems may be infinitely varied, but the facing of problems does not alter. And the facing of cultural problems illustrates a recurrent pattern. The history of human thought, and the history of philosophical ideas in particular, exhibits with unusual clarity the general structure of social and cultural change. This fact made a tremendous impression on Hegel. He was led to base his comprehensive philosophy upon it, to attempt to set forth how the course of man's philosophizing looks to God. He and his Marxian followers have called that pattern the "dialectic" of history. Now the structure of cultural conflict and change, and its expression and articulation in man's philosophizing, may or may not be properly called "dialectical." The answer most philosophic analysis today would give, is that it may not. But it remains true that it is impossible to gain any insight into the history of philosophical ideas—into the historical dimensions of philosophizing—without being led to formulate a philosophy of cultural change.

The history of philosophical ideas is both cumulative and original. Ideas seized upon because they meet the needs generated by one type of experience have a structure and implications and entailments of their own. That structure can be followed out, explored and pushed, by men who have the intellectual interest and motive, and who are not led to stop short in their exploring by the pressure of practical involvement in some particular conflict, because they have come upon an idea that will serve their immediate intellectual ends.

But men are always far more concerned to use ideas than to understand them. And when other elements in their culture, perhaps only remotely connected with those ideas, have developed so far as to bring into existence another type of social experience, men come to feel the need of turning to new ideas. So out of the fragments of previous structures and complexes, they set out to build a new one. Intellectually, in our own culture there has been a genuine continuity of materials, carried along in what we shall have to examine carefully, its several philosophical traditions. But there has been no orderly progress, no simple fixed line of development moving through time, no unilinear "evolution." Ideas have had, rather, adventurous careers, like the complexes we call "traditions" in which they come embedded. There has been rather a succession of lootings of the past by each new present. No great philosophy has ever been "refuted." It has rather been discarded as irrelevant, irrelevant to another newly emerged type of intellectual and cultural experience. The system of Aristotle was not refuted by the gospels of the Hellenistic schools that followed after it in time. Rather, the need for deliverance, for a way of salvation, grew more pressing than the Aristotelian desire to understand. The imposing medieval syntheses, Arabic, Jewish, or Christian, were never refuted by the scientific humanitarianisms to which men in search of emancipation turned. Rather, men came to feel other values more insistent than the intellectual and spiritual values they had enabled men to secure. And if the scientific and humanistic philosophies of our own time are destined to be superseded by other and more dogmatic views of nature and human society, it will not be because they have been "disproved." It will be only because they have been for the time being made irrelevant, by our intense need for social direction and military security, even at the sacrifice of the searching mind and the critical temper.

We have been emphasizing the cultural functions of philosophic thinking. Those functions were found to be essentially critical. Confronted by a cultural, or culturally significant social, conflict between men's beliefs, the philosophical mind —that is, the mind in which such conflicts generate a philosophical response—is driven to examine the fundamental beliefs that underlie the clusters of beliefs that have come to collide. It gives special consideration to the new ideas, generated by a fresh intellectual experience, that seem, on the surface at least, to be inconsistent with the familiar ideas in terms of which men have been leading their intellectual lives, and which have served to organize their beliefs into a reasonably coherent whole.

During modern times, these new ideas have come normally from fresh scientific formulations. They have been such propositions as, the notion that the earth goes round the sun; that nature is at bottom a system or order of particles of matter in motion, whose activities can be described and handled in mathematical terms; that the supposedly immutable species of living things are all descended from one, or at least a few, common ancestors; that the available energy in the universe is tending toward a form in which it will not be usable for sustaining any form of life; that particles of matter are not ultimate, indivisible "atoms," but are complex systems of radiant energy illustrating complicated mathematical formulae; that man's soul is not a simple substance, but the activities of a complexly organized physical body; that man's intelligence and reason are the devices of an unconscious but calculating urge or impulse whose aims are irrelevant to man's conscious ends.

All these ideas, worked out in the institution of science, that during the modern period has come to be the distinctive mark and possession of our Western culture, and has for almost a century been eagerly snatched at by the more enlightened minds of other cultures, have generated philosophic responses, and have led to the erection of imposing philosophies, and to the elaboration of sharp and penetrating methods of criticism. It is such ideas with which philosophic thinking, aroused by their contrast with the familiar inherited beliefs that used to make things so clear, has felt itself compelled to come to terms.

Philosophers have never agreed on just how to meet any of these crises, and the various ways they have on each occasion explored have normally been in rivalry and competition with each other. But if thinkers have never all agreed on the solution, and have diverged the more widely, as the novel idea that set them off was the more disturbing and life-shaking, they have normally been in agreement on the central intellectual problem which at that time must be faced.

Those who have demurred have been those whose beliefs were so strongly held and so tightly organized that even the problems that still seemed most important to them were themselves inherited, the now traditional problems which had originally led to the working out of those beliefs now so tenaciously held. There are always around representatives of such philosophies that have grown, as we say, "academic," because even their problems as well as their concepts and methods have survived unchanged from an earlier day. They do not feel the challenge of a Copernicus, a Newton, a Darwin, or a Freud, they do not find the impact of the novel ideas such names symbolize to be a challenge to their own philosophizing, because the fresh ideas for them can make no impact. They have more familiar, more important, and more traditional problems with which to deal.

But though during the modern period it has been revolutions in scientific concepts and methods that have been the most disruptive, and hence the major stimulus to new philosophizing, such disruptions and intellectual reconstructions of beliefs have been carried on against the background of the slower but even more deep-seated changes in Western society. Fresh social experience has been as ultimately controlling in setting the problems of philosophic thinking as revolutionary ideas in science. Normally, such novel social experience has not impinged with the breath-taking suddenness of the new world of the H-bomb, or of the revolt of Asia and Africa from centuries of European domination. But since the tenth century our expanding Western society has seen the development of technological, economic, and political institutions which have been slowly but steadily outgrowing the older forms of social organization inherited from the earlier Middle Ages and before. These emerging institutions have demanded above all liberation from the older frameworks that had once served reasonably well. They have slowly but with steadily increasing insistence come to generate new activities, and hence new ends and, as we say, new values, often irrelevant to the older social aims, often in definite opposition to them. And so they have stimulated certain philosophic minds to explore, and to defend, these emerging values, and certain others to seek a surer foundation for the traditional values they in turn are anxious to defend and support.

Normally, the really outstanding philosophers have been challenged to effect a deeper synthesis, in which the values of old and new alike would be brought together and adjusted. But there have always been those philosophers who have managed to express the *Zeitgeist*, to ride the crest of new demands for social organization, and new social values, that after long germination in quiet were just on the point of being recognized and eagerly embraced. John Locke, with some injustice to the penetration and wide horizon of his own complex thinking, is conventionally, and with some reason, taken as the symbol of this second kind of thinker, the man who could ride the crest of the popular Whig wave down through the American Revolution. Immanuel Kant, the much more complex expression of a much more complicated wave, or line of breakers, is another. Only in his third critique did he really face the future. In the first and second he summed up, as we say, the "living tendencies of his age."

In contrast, there are always philosophers of the first type, the synthesizers of the old with the new. They are naturally regarded as either "behind" or "ahead of" their time, for they are normally both. Hobbes embraced eagerly the new science of Galileo, not yet come to general acceptance. He expressed also the demand for strong central government, able to crush the opposition of a decadent feudalism and a still vital conflict of spiritual and secular powers. This demand had underlain the long-continued surge toward what we call "Renaissance despotism," a surge that in England had already passed its peak. Hobbes at the same time gave rational form to the older Augustinian and the newer Calvinistic and Puritan distrust of human nature. This low estimate of man's powers linked him to the earlier reaction against high medieval complacency and optimism, but was already a lost cause in view of the rising faith in rational man. Out of these ingredients, old and new, Hobbes managed to forge a fresh vision of man in the body politic. His cool vision was to lend itself admirably to the modern religion of the state. But Hobbes really rose to an insight more classic than modern, more eternal than temporally limited, of what man must do to be saved in the modern world of body in motion.

Or there is Spinoza, most eternal of philosophers. He likewise in the full seventeenth century retained a passionate devotion to all the medieval values. Yet at the same time he seems a startling foreshadowing of that liberal "pantheism" that was to dominate so much of nineteenth-century thinking. In the midst of conservative Dutch constitutionalism he worked out a tolerant democracy that came into its own only with Rousseau and the French Revolution. Yet he did it to provide the social setting within which man might be saved from human bondage to the passions through union with God. He too was both behind, and ahead of, his times.

The intellectual history of the West reveals the same story repeated over and over. New ideas, from science or from a changing social experience, impinge upon the older inherited ideas and seem to be in logical conflict with them. These conflicts, when socially significant enough to affect a considerable part of society, or at least the intellectual class, present new and insistent problems of adjustment and assimilation. They challenge thinkers to explore the bearing of the new issues upon the old, throughout all the institutions of culture. This necessitates a careful intellectual clarification and criticism. Normally the process culminates in a reconstruction of both new and old. It was this process that Hegel turned to, from which to generalize his philosophy of cultural change. Out of it he pulled, as his *Jugendschriften* make clear, the main pattern of his "dialectic," before he dressed it up in rigid logical categories. For us, Hegel has probably ruined any possible "dialectic" of intellectual history. But we can still speak of a "dialogue" in which the future asks questions of the past embodied in the present, and the present replies—by generating a new philosophy.

To vary the figure, we can see the philosopher at his humblest as the politician of ideas, by his deals and compromises effecting a working agreement to live and let live, so that thinking may go on. Such a familiar process does not normally give birth to an imposing new philosophy. But all the same it transforms the old one within whose notions and methods men continue to operate. Think of the slow transformation of political "liberalism" from Finality Jack Russell of the Reform Bill of 1832 to the program of the New Deal and of the Americans for Democratic Action. Here is a long line of politicians of the mind who over the generations effected this reconstruction of ideas in the light of changing social experience and needs. We rarely dignify this succession with the name of "philosophers." But, culturally speaking, this was a genuine, not to say an essential, philosophical function.

At his proudest the philosopher is the statesman of ideas, constructing in his novel synthesis a new constitutional framework within which men can henceforth conduct their altered lines of thinking. This is the more imaginative and creative function of the philosopher: it involves a more personal perspective and often a more private accent. At its most impressive, it leads to the erection of one of those great architectonic edifices of ideas that can give us a perspective on all time and all eternity. But even such imaginative expressions of the wisdom of an organized culture must be set upon the solid foundation of an adjustment or synthesis between old and new. We think of a Thomas Aquinas, consummate adjuster, and creator of a still living imaginative vision. Or we consider an Aristotle, whose synthesis of all the earlier intellectual explorations of the eager Greek mind could dominate for two millennia the imagination of Greeks, Moslems, and Western Latins alike. The philosopher-statesman, the thinker in whom speculative power—the power to look upon what is—is added to critical acumen—the power to make it all fit together—is the man who can work out a newer and more inclusive idea, which will embrace the warring beliefs, and accord them both intellectual justice. He effects his philosophical reconstruction by generalizing some idea, usually taken from a particular field, and using it to transmute both sets of clashing beliefs. Thus, to reconcile the insights of the pre-Parmenidean Greeks, of the atomists, and of the later Plato, Aristotle seized upon the idea of dynamic process. He saw that things must be able to do what they obviously can do, before they do it, that the actual is the operation or exercise of the potential. He derived the idea from the study of the subject-matter of biology, from living things and above all from the life of man. To reconcile the wisdom of the Greeks with the knowledge of the moderns, and to give mathematical formulation to Aristotle's world of dynamic processes, Leibniz generalized the root idea of the calculus, the formula or law governing an infinitesimal series. He drew upon his mathematical discovery of the calculus. Hegel brought man's world of social institutions together with his knowledge of nature, through the idea of evolution, which he took from the cultural history of human societies.

It is from such a generalizing of ideas in the face of a new problem of intellectual adjustment, that the greatest philosophies spring. Consider Plato. He confronted the conflict that had arisen among the Sophists, between those who saw all that was best in men's institutions and lives dependent on *nomos*, on "law," on what men do in their cities and communities, and those who, like Socrates, looked rather to *physis*, to man's nature itself, as rooted in the cosmic *physis* or nature. He turned to the highest achievement of Greek science, geometry, for help. There, in geometrical form, he found something in nature on which to model law, something in which the mind could rest assured, and toward which love could safely be directed. Those without the imaginative insight to generalize ideas do not become the supreme philosophical geniuses. Nor do their insights, however fruitful in particular fields, solve cultural conflicts and continue to dominate the activities of the mind.

For such edifices can continue to serve thinking, long beyond the particular conflict that presided at their erection. They rise above the special problem of intellectual adjustment to gain a vision of what is. They achieve a perspective upon the enduring traits of the world and of man's manifold encounters with it. They formulate the ultimate distinctions in terms of which men must acknowledge what is and discriminate what they must love. These distinctions take their place in an emerging metaphysics, an emerging ontology. They were first formulated by the Greeks in their brave attempt to get behind the religious cosmogonies they had inherited from the Mesopotamian and Egyptian world, an attempt turned into conflicts by the long struggle between *logos* and *nomos*, between reason and tradition. They have been slowly added to in the subsequent history of the West. These distinctions have been both forced upon men, and refined and extended, by the long wrestling with the historical problems of cultural adjustment. Again and again men have been driven back to the same distinctions in deepened form by the oppositions they have confronted. For metaphysical inquiry, like all scientific inquiry, is fundamentally historical in character: it is cumulative and progressive. One need read only a page of Aristotle to see how his metaphysical distinctions grew out of a long previous wrestling of those whom he calls *hoi archaioi*, "the ancients." And one needs only the slightest acquaintance with the course of modern philosophy, from Descartes's analytic geometry to the theory of relativity and the field, to realize how nearly all the novel ideas of the metaphysics of modern times have grown out of the impingement of fresh scientific experience. The concepts and distinctions have been enlarged and deepened. But in a significant sense, our present philosophies can still be classed as fundamentally Platonic or Aristotelian. The intellectual edifices that the great philosophers of the past builded have a way of enduring.

II. Historical Patterns in Philosophical Traditions

I have been speaking of the complex process which has been the intellectual life of Western culture. I have been emphasizing the most general pattern it exhibits to the inquiring mind, the pattern of confrontation of the novel, assimilation, adjustment, and subsequent reconstruction. This seems to be the pattern of intellectual change and growth in general. We could pursue it further, as great philosophies of cultural change have tried to pursue it. We could ask where new scientific ideas come from, and examine in detail the rather erratic course of scientific inquiry. Auguste Comte attempted such an intellectual interpretation of cultural history; but his three stages through which all ideas pass, theological, metaphysical, and positivistic, were painted with far too broad a brush for much intellectual illumination.

We could ask where new social ideas emerge, like those of inalienable rights, or of democracy, and we should be led into the details of institutional development. Here in our day we should encounter the imposing historical philosophy of Karl Marx. Marx, deeply concerned with promoting a political revolution, saw such revolutions occurring when the economic organization of a society—its "relations of production" —have outgrown the political organization for controlling and directing them, and lead men to demand a change in political institutions, to bring the two more closely into line.

The form of economic organization he saw as in turn dependent on the state of technology—on the "forces of production" —and the state of technology itself as dependent on the state of knowledge, of science. The initiator of social change—the ultimate "dynamic"—is thus knowledge and science, the discovery a society makes of how to do something new.

But men are consciously driven to seek social change—they demand a "revolution"—only when technology has made the old economic organization obsolete, and an obstruction. Changes in the economic organization can be effected, however, only by changes in the scheme of political control. So men formulate their demands for economic change in terms of political ideals. Social change is thus ultimately initiated by new scientific and technological discoveries. But it can be consciously directed only through the political instruments for changing the economic organization. Hence men's social ideals and social philosophies are brought to a focus on the capture of the instruments of political power; they are the "ideologies" of the warring economic classes seeking control of the ultimate means of directing the economy.

Now, this philosophy of social change was wonderfully illuminating when Marx first propounded it. It has left its mark upon all our subsequent philosophies of institutional history. It certainly helps at least to explain why new social ideas have emerged when they have. It points to the inescapable element of "ideology," of serving as a political instrument for getting men to work together to do what has to be done, or to resist the doing as long as possible, that marks most of the philosophies of the modern period, especially those that have been socially influential, like British empiricism or German *Staatsphilosophie*.

But like all philosophies that ride the wave and express the needs of the moment, the lessons of Marxism have been so taken to heart that men have proceeded to alter the conditions it began by exhibiting. Having learned that political programs are dependent on disputes about directing and organizing the economy, men have concentrated on the political instruments, until today it is doubtful whether political organization "depends on" economic organization, or economic on political. In all industrial lands the "working classes" of Marx's analysis have through democratic political instruments already "captured the State," and are administering it with a view to their interests. In the "underdeveloped" countries, including Russia, it is the political organization that is really creating the forces of production, and setting up an economy for an emerging industry and for agriculture. Indeed, the Marxist analysis seems to retain its validity only for those periods before men had learned the lessons of Marx. Foreseeing the inevitable future Marx predicted, men listening to his wisdom have set about preventing it. Perhaps this is a good definition of an "ideology," that it is a prediction whose acceptance makes unnecessary or impossible its fulfillment. The Marxian philosophy seems to be a classic example.

With its concentration on preparing another political revolution, the Marxian philosophy of cultural change, we now realize, was also a greatly simplified picture of the complex pattern of that process. New political and social ideas have emerged not only as the formulation of economic demands, though in the modern world they have never emerged without that context. Majority rule, and the reserved constitutional rights of individuals and groups, did not come merely from economic conflicts. In point of fact, they sprang just as much from the conflicts between secular and religious powers. Liberty and equality were the demands of persecuted churches that rose in revolt, as much as of merchants trying to make ends meet or overlap. The passion for God has been quite as strong a human motive as the passion for gold—even when both have disturbed the lives of the same men. And it has been much harder to deny God's rights than those of gold. God and gold acting together created our modern political world, just as justice and power are remaking today the worlds of Asia and Africa. Such marriages of seeming incompatibles can be strong and endure. On the whole, in shaping our American political philosophy, Calvin has been quite as influential as Calvin Coolidge, and Adam's sin as Adam Smith. Even for his own revolutionary aims, Marx underestimated the power and importance of religion, as in their several ways the British Labour Party and the Catholic Church can still make clear. At times religion may serve as the opiate of the people. But just as often it turns out to be their benzedrin.

It is well not to underestimate the extent to which our social and moral philosophies have been "ideologies," instruments for predicting the future so that we might alter the inevitable. But with them the situation seems analogous to what we have found with our scientific philosophies. In the latter case, the edifices of ideas springing from a particular problem of intellectual adjustment have nevertheless been forced to achieve a broader perspective, and to contribute to the illumination of a perennial metaphysics, an emerging pattern of what is and what must be accepted. Can it not be that in our social philosophies of freedom and individuality and democratic equality, we have also been working toward more than immediate advantage, toward standards of more universal validity—standards by which to judge our imperfect achievement?

In the old days, men had inherited from the Cynics and the

Stoics through the Roman jurists and the canonists of the Church the notion of such a binding "law of nature." Men like Grotius and Pufendorf and Locke and Quesnay did indeed turn it into an ideological instrument in the particular revolutionary demands of the seventeenth and eighteenth centuries. And since Hume we have been all too aware of the difficulties in the whole idea. Our historians have made clear the extent to which this natural law of the Western tradition was limited and far from universal, even could we be persuaded to take it as obligatory. But have we not actually been working toward more universal standards? Is our devotion to human freedom as much a mere ideology as our devotion to "free enterprise" obviously is? If in its defense we are seriously prepared to destroy the world, it would be well to give the matter some thought.

We could ask such questions about the pattern of cultural change, and the attempts of philosophers to illuminate it. We could doubt the clear over-simplifications of a Comte or a Marx, even as we recognize that in asking where the new ideas that provoke philosophies come from, they were raising important questions. One thing at least is clear: they do not come from philosophy itself, they come from philosophic reflection on a changing intellectual and social world. If Hegel actually thought that it is *Vernunft* that creates new ideas, and even the occasion of their creation, he is not very illuminating. We should still have to inquire, what is it in *Vernunft* that leads it to bring forth such novel offspring? To explain anything in the world as the creation of God—which with the right understanding of God and of creation may well be true enough, and of great importance for the religious life—is to throw no real light on its specific method of genesis, until we know far more of God's processes of creating than we know as yet. The categories of Hegel's *Logik*—to avoid controversy I shall not call it his "logic"—are of no help.

Even for the dialectician, *Logik* of itself tells us nothing about what in particular is being "negated," and nothing about any new "synthesis," until we have observed what that synthesis is, or discovered it in a larger context. Just what is the "negation" of capitalism? We are all of us, Communists and "capitalists" alike, still trying to work that out. Have we already "negated" the conditions of the working-class in England in 1844, that Engels so graphically described? The answer is clear. Have we "negated" capitalism? I strongly suspect we have, all over the world, if "capitalism" is what Marx described as he saw it about him in Victorian England. Have we achieved a new "synthesis"? I doubt it as yet, even—I trust and hope—even in the classic land of socialism. No, new ideas do not come from philosophy. They come from working with the materials our world offers us.

Much the same difficulty may be raised about the "history of ideas" of Arthur O. Lovejoy. He is not so pretentious as Hegel, and he does not claim that new ideas come from a *Weltvernunft*. He does not know where they come from; he is much more interested in exploring what they are, than in raising that question, which he thinks is as yet unanswerable. He classifies and distinguishes ideas, without troubling over the pattern of their development. Mr. Lovejoy may be attractively modest, but he leaves the history of ideas as something self-contained and autonomous, just as Hegel does. At most, philosophy, in which the new ideas first appear, is something expansive: they push out from there into literature, into architecture, and even into gardening.

As a matter of fact, in the course of some effort spent on

exploring the processes of cultural change, I have been led to mark the occurrence of many historical patterns of various types, patterns in the careers of philosophical ideas. These different types of historical pattern, which I have been forced to recognize as illustrated over and over again, are characteristic of different strands in the philosophic enterprise. They are subordinate patterns of intellectual change, sometimes found within, sometimes cutting across the major strands of assimilation.

These historical patterns to which my attention has been called, are purely empirical generalizations. About them is no dialectical necessity that I have been able to discover. There is not the mysterious psychological necessity that Spengler found in *The Decline of the West,* nor even the kinds of teleological necessity that may be lurking in Toynbee, who likewise claims merely to be making empirical generalizations. They are not derivable from any unifying law or formula of intellectual history. I have not succeeded in drawing them together into any kind of unified system: they are plural and, so far as I have found, unrelated. But they seem to be repeatedly exemplified. What may be the conditions of that exemplification, which, if changed, would lead to the presence of another pattern, I have hardly endeavored to inquire. But they all illustrate the presence of historical continuities in philosophizing. They all illuminate the historical dimensions of philosophy. They all contribute to the understanding of philosophic ideas, when their presence is noted. It is certain of these historical patterns that I now want to select for delineation and comment.

First, I want to select the pattern of the historical process of criticism we call "metaphysical," that fundamental kind of criticism which appeals from some intellectual formulation to experience as actually lived or enjoyed "directly" or "immediately." In such metaphysical criticism, the philosopher criticizes some formulated scheme of understanding, some "abstraction" from the encountered world, some theory, some concept, some distinction that has grown into a "dualism," by appealing to a fuller and richer "experience"—to the world actually encountered in all the varied ways in which men do encounter it in their various human enterprises.

Such criticism is the most fundamental kind, more fundamental than the criticism that finds an idea not internally self-consistent, or logically inconsistent with other ideas we are prepared to accept unquestioningly. Such logical inconsistencies are easily detectable; by making the proper distinctions, they are not too difficult to overcome. When for any reason the mind is anxious and eager to hold simultaneously to two ideas that on the surface appear logically inconsistent, it is not hard to distinguish senses, or to embrace them both in a more fundamental idea. The wit of man has again and again turned the trick; the history of resolving conflicts between new and old ideas is full of illustrations.

But it is a far more serious matter to find an idea in conflict with the deliverances of experience. Some philosophers, indeed, are hardy and brazen enough to meet such a situation with the disdainful remark, "So much the worse for experience!" Of them Parmenides is the father. From the days of Copernicus he has enjoyed a distant progeny among modern philosophers, encouraged by the fact that scientists have so often told us the world is not really what it seems. Missing the fact that the scientists have been correcting common opinion in order ultimately to "save the appearances" more carefully ascertained, they have taken this as license to deny what seems to be so. The classic instance is the "subjective idealism" Berkeley is conventionally supposed to have initiated—though in actual fact he is no "subjective idealist," and an "idealist" at all only in that he employed the "new way of ideas" of Locke to establish the realism of common sense. But the record of modern philosophy is full of those resolute minds who have come to conceive some scheme of intelligibility, some narrow conception of what is "rational," and have condemned all ordinary experience because it fails to come up to the mark. Phenomenalism, which so bravely insists it will accept no belief not founded on "impressions" derived from "experience," can claim to be a genuine philosophy of experience only if "experience" be actually what it confidently assumes it must be. As an empirical philosophy, it founders on the fact that metaphysical criticism can easily show that man's actual experience is miles removed from what phenomenalism assumes its "experience" must be.

Perhaps the Kantians have been most successful at this game, because most sophisticated, in their insistence that schemes of intelligibility cannot be criticized by any appeal to experience, because they are first assumed and applied to determine what "experience" can be. The canons of scientific method and intelligibility determine what can be taken as scientific experience—"possible experience," they call it. This is true enough for science, and well argued, for example, in Cassirer's *Substance and Function*. But Kant himself was the first to recognize that men then find themselves enjoying many kinds and forms of experience that extend beyond the limits of scientific or "possible" experience. And in occupying himself with trying to make sense, in terms of his own scheme of intelligibility, of moral experience and of the experiences of beauty and of artistic creation, he opened the gates to the exploration of all these many varieties of human *Erlebnis* that are not illuminated by confining *Erfahrung* to *Empfindung* and *Vorstellungen*.*

If the scheme of scientific intelligibility, or the "categories of the understanding," determine what can pass as scientific experience, or "pure reason," then scientific experience must itself be placed in its setting of all the other forms of *Erlebnis*, and "pure reason" must be seen as only one form of "transcendental reason." This step the Romanticists took, and set about exploring the length and breadth of man's *Erlebnis*. Hegel crowned their enterprise by undertaking a "phenomenology" of all human culture, assigning each form and enterprise its own place in the totality of human experience completely understood. He also took the inevitable step of criticizing Kant's "pure" or "abstract" reason, in the light of the "concrete" reason of man's social and cultural experience, which is fundamentally historical in character. Hegel was the supreme reconciler, synthesizer, and reconstructor of the nineteenth century. As such, his edifice lies behind all the later developments of nineteenth-century social science, just as Kant's adjustment lies behind all developments in the natural sciences.

Hegel phrased his "phenomenological criticism" as the "critique of abstractions" in the light of their function in experience. This is what I have been calling "metaphysical criticism;" the Germans and the Continentals in general now call it "phenomenological criticism." It dominates all serious philosophizing today, as we shall see in the next chapter. It

---

* A working Kantian lexicon, that to be sure misses many of the all-important connotations, might run: *Erlebnis* is "direct experience"; *Erfahrung* is "experience" in the most general sense; *Empfindung* is "sensation" or "feeling"; *Vorstellungen* are "sense-impressions."

is exemplified in the philosophers of the early twentieth century, F. H. Bradley, William James, John Dewey, Henri Bergson, A. N. Whitehead, Edmund Husserl, Martin Heidegger; and today in the logical positivists, the followers of Wittgenstein, the Continental phenomenologists and existentialists, and the American experimental naturalists. A method of criticism so important and so widely followed by philosophers starting from a variety of specific problems of adjustment, deserves careful consideration of the historical pattern these enterprises of criticism have illustrated.

But Hegel, in criticizing Kant's—and Newton's—"abstract reason," did not initiate metaphysical or phenomenological criticism of schemes of intelligibility. Aristotle began it, as he began so many enterprises that Hegel carried on in the atmosphere of post-Kantian Romanticism. Aristotle invented what we call "metaphysics," and what he himself called "first philosophy," to criticize the "separation" by the Platonists of intelligible form or structure from the world of natural things or ordinary experience. Their separation of form he criticized by calling attention to the world of natural processes "we see" about us, from which the Platonists in their mathematical enthusiasm had "abstracted" their forms. It was not their genuine insight into forms, but the abstraction, that Aristotle was criticizing. He too, we remember, was a synthesizer and reconstructor, who tried to preserve the best of the Platonists' insight. Aristotle in fact is the first and still the most successful of that long line of philosophers who in the Western tradition have tried to harmonize the conflicting visions of Platonism and Aristotelianism—unless we reserve the priority for the author of the *Dialogues* himself. For Plato the dramatist—whatever may have been true of Plato the professor in the

Academy—was, like Aristotle, a harmonizer of Platonism and Aristotelianism.

In our own day John Dewey is speaking as the heir of both the Aristotelian and the Hegelian traditions, when he calls metaphysics the "ground-plan of criticism," the criticism of those schemes of scientific intelligibility which are themselves methods of criticizing the beliefs of mankind. Such criticism has had a history from Aristotle to Dewey and Husserl and Heidegger and the rest today. Its temporal pattern is thus worth considering.

In the first place, such metaphysical or phenomenological criticism always sets out from some determinate formulated scheme of understanding that prevails in the critic's culture. The critic appeals to more "concrete" and "direct" experience, to what "we see," as Aristotle put it. But he does not appeal to it to remain with "experience as lived." He appeals, like Hegel, to get a more adequate formulation, to find an enlarged scheme of intelligibility.

Historically considered, the appeal to "experience" is never the first step in philosophizing. In any concrete enterprise of criticism, the concept of "experience" is not the starting-point, not a "datum," but an instrument of criticism. This is just the difference between a method that is "empirical" in the narrow sense, and one that is genuinely "experimental." "Empirical" method professes to start from the "immediate deliverances of experience," however they be conceived. But in such a method experience is never approached "immediately"; it has already been conceived in terms of some antecedent scheme of analysis. It is just at this point that the assumptions inherited from a tradition enter in. In contrast, "experimental" method is much closer to recognizing the actual procedure of thinking: it always starts frankly from a whole antecedent body of ideas. It approaches experience not only with some hypothesis to be confirmed or criticized; for experience or observation can serve the function of "evidence" only in connection with some specific hypothesis. Still more, experimental method assumes to begin with the funded body of knowledge already acquired in the past. There can be no experimental method except in the context of an already tested store of beliefs and ideas.

So the start of the appeal to experience is always with some codified experience of nature already won, some understanding already achieved of nature, some knowledge previously acquired. Men appeal to experience only to criticize this assumed understanding of nature, in order to get a better understanding of nature; in the process, incidentally, they acquire an enlarged and deepened conception of experience itself. As an historical pattern, the process runs: from experience we have derived some conception of nature. From that conception we appeal to experience afresh to get an enlarged conception of nature. That in turn modifies our ideas as to what experience is and can be, and the new conception won of experience makes it possible to criticize again our notion of nature. And so on. Is this a paradox? No, it seems to be the natural course of metaphysical criticism and inquiry.

Historically, there thus appears a pattern of passing back and forth from nature to experience to nature to experience, and to nature again. On a large scale, we encounter in the record periods in which the predominant emphasis is critical, and other periods of what we call "synthetic achievement." Since the eighteenth century, our philosophical movements have been fundamentally critical: we have seen the successive critical appeals to experience of Kant, of the Romanticists, of Hegel, of the post-Darwinian philosophies of experience in which we are living today. For we can learn from experience only if we have already learned something from experience. For the concepts by which we make fresh experience intelligible, the ultimately intelligible values we are seeking, the standards by which we verify, are themselves the deposit of a long experience with the world. To the test of this embodied experience we bring our newly gained experience. In the testing, the tests are themselves tested, and the outcome left as a new deposit. What we have already learned teaches us to ask questions better; and in the asking, we learn how to ask still better ones.

This can be summed up by saying, that for inquiry and criticism the "immediate" is never given, and that the appeal to experience is no starting-point, but an intermediate stage in the process of criticizing the reflective experience we do actually start with, that is, the experienced world already formulated in some scheme of interpretation. The pattern of the history of our successive philosophies of experience exhibits this in detail. Thus Hegel criticized the "abstract universals" of Enlightenment rationalism and of Kant, in terms of the "concrete universal" revealed by his phenomenology of experience. Kierkegaard criticizes the Hegelian philosophy of "essence," in the light of human "existence." The post-Hegelians criticize the "intellectualism" of the Hegelian tradition in the light of "life," in the *Lebensphilosophie* of Nietzsche and Dilthey. Husserl and his phenomenological followers criticize the formalism of the Neo-Kantians, from Lange to Cassirer, in the light of a new description of actual experience. The *Existenzphilosophie* of Heidegger and Jaspers, and Paul Tillich, criticizes the formalism of Husserl. Bergson criticizes the "t" of physics in the light of the "duration" of concretely intuited experience. Bradley criticizes appearance as consisting of abstractions, since only the whole is concrete and real. He and William James appeal to immediate experience to criticize the formulated and abstract "experience" of traditional empiricism. Dewey criticized the refined experience of the sciences and of philosophic schemes, by pointing to or denoting experience in the gross, macroscopic or direct experience. Whitehead criticizes the abstractions of Newtonian science by appealing to the immediate deliverances of sense-awareness.

In the second place, such a critical appeal to experience attempts always to take into account everything man finds in his experienced world. As Woodbridge puts it, "In passing beyond the limits of the evident situation in which man finds himself, we must not neglect anything within that situation," as evidence for the nature of its context. Historically, this is of course a counsel of perfection. Just such neglect is the reason for the long search for the "given," for what is supposedly there "to begin with"; such search is undertaken when the consequences of neglecting some particular factor are causing trouble in reflective experience, because they have led to conclusions in some scheme of science or philosophy which are clashing with other ideas. Thus it is always a specific neglect causing trouble, that initiates fresh metaphysical criticism. It sends men back to the "evident situation" in which mankind finds itself—to the "immediate" or "direct" experience of Dewey, to the "intuition of essences" of Santayana, to the phenomenological inquiry of Husserl, to the human *Existenz* of Heidegger and Jaspers, to the intuition of reality of Bergson, to the inquiry into being of Maritain.

So these are all illustrations of what is at bottom the same critical enterprise. Each of these thinkers has been impressed by some specific neglect in previous formulations of reflective experience. None is able, of course, to free himself from all his own inherited assumptions. None is able to escape all previous interpretation. None is able to discover bare "fact." All of them are controlled by their own philosophical traditions, by the familiar categories of language they take for granted, by the uncriticized assumptions left standing because they are not immediately relevant to the specific neglect the critic is trying to remedy. This is at least clear of the "evident situations" that are appealed to—by everybody else. And only historical knowledge can reveal what the critic who is appealing to bare experience is actually taking for granted, and why he is continuing to assume it without question.

But in the process, in each case certain neglected factors are actually revealed. That is why the pattern of metaphysical criticism is historical, and why we can speak of "progress" in metaphysical inquiry. The pattern has in fact been cumulative and cooperative, like that of any other scientific inquiry; it illustrates what we were distinguishing as the "experimental method" which seems to be the actual procedure of how we think. That is true even when, as is so often the case, the particular interpretation of the neglected factors freshly discovered proves ultimately unacceptable. The factor itself is there to be fitted in more plausibly with men's other ideas. Thus Bergson called attention to "duration," or "real time," and thus initiated the era of "taking time seriously." His own interpretation of duration has been rejected. But there has ever since been a pervasive temporalism running through all the major metaphysical formulations. In all of them time is taken seriously, even when by elaborate argument the philosopher tries to convince us that time ought not to be taken seriously. He has at any rate to give serious consideration to

the reasons for his metaphysical conservatism in rejecting the
new idea.

The pattern of metaphysical criticism, then, is revealed by
the historical record as, like that of all scientific inquiry, progressive, never finished, never reaching final conclusions. I
remember an occasion on which this fact of metaphysical life
had been pointed out by an American. A philosopher of Teu-
tonic extraction arose to ask, "Then you mean that philosophy
reaches no more and no greater certainty than physics, for
example?" John Dewey was in the audience. He got up,
smiled his inimitable smile, and repeated, with emphasis, "No
greater certainty than *physics*?" Anyone who can find that a
serious objection, is obviously not interested in philosophical
inquiry. Such a man is clearly looking for a faith.

There is in philosophy another type of historical continuity
which exhibits within itself historical patterns of change and
growth, characteristic and repeatedly exemplified, as one sur-
veys the past history of philosophic thinking in the Western
world. This type is one which, as I have studied the record
and attempted to explore some of its complicated and inter-
twined strands, has come to assume increasing importance,
and to be indeed the key to untangling the patterns of historical change. This is the notion of a "philosophical tradition," a
persistent body of ideas tied together by subtle associations
as well as by logical relations, which persists over the generations, and dominates and colors the thinking of those who
for one reason or another have been brought up in it.

A philosophical tradition is that type of historical continuity
which enjoys a career, in the sense that its course—its "life,"
one is tempted to say—can be traced from the beginning,

through the various vicissitudes it has undergone as men have
turned to it and worked with it in facing and trying to deal
with their specific problems of adjustment. Such a tradition
starts usually with the achievement of the kind of thinker
we have called a "philosophical statesman"; it is his comprehensive thought that is launched for others to work with. In
the West these traditions have for the most part started with
the pioneer Greeks. But the traditions the Western world
inherited from the Greek thinkers and schools have been
carried on, worked with, applied to new cultural conflicts and
problems, as men's intellectual and social experience has altered, and reconstructed again and again as a result of how
they have been modified and added to in facing new problems.
Whenever philosophic thinking has been vital, and not merely
inherited, such traditions have been transformed. But certain
of their features persist, and enable us to identify them as later
stages of the same tradition. Much like the career of a man, we
may say they exhibit a continuing identity of personality.

Such a philosophic tradition is defined and rendered a persistent identity, by certain characteristic assumptions which
thinkers in it continue to make as a matter of course without
questioning. These assumptions are varied: they are assumptions as to starting point, as to method, as to the ultimate distinctions to make, as to certain concepts to be employed, as to
certain "positions" to be defended. These assumptions differ
also in what we can call their "toughness" and their amena-
bility to criticism. In any tradition, some assumptions are
much more superficial than others. The record shows that
they can be criticized and modified again and again, by a
thoroughgoing critical mind. But often even these more
superficial assumptions appear in the next generation as taken

without questioning again. It is really surprising how the assumptions of British empiricism, for example, as formulated by Locke, are repeated by men like James and John Stuart Mill, or in our own day by Bertrand Russell, long after they have been fundamentally criticized and transformed by acute minds like David Hume, or Whitehead. Other assumptions in the same tradition are much more deep-seated, and are never questioned, even by minds as penetrating as Hume's or Whitehead's. It is these clusters of assumptions, both the more superficial and the more deep-seated, that later philosophers appeal to in dealing with the obvious problems of intellectual conflict that confront them, problems usually generated in modern times, we have seen, by a new scheme of scientific understanding.

The classic example of the persistence of philosophical traditions occurs in that century that fancied it was making the greatest intellectual break with the past, and was henceforth wholly on its own, the seventeenth—that century of "intellectual pioneers," as Whitehead has called it. Confronted by the overwhelming new intellectual fact of the mathematical interpretation of nature, all the major seventeenth-century philosophical "pioneers" turned to one or another of the three philosophical traditions inherited from the late Middle Ages: to the Augustinian philosophy of knowledge and science, like Descartes and the Cartesians; to the realistic Aristotelianism of Thomas and the anticlerical Italian schools, like Galileo, Spinoza, and Leibniz; and to the nominalistic Aristotelianism of William of Ockham and the Terminists, like Hobbes, Locke, and Newton. The seventeenth-century philosophers turned to these late medieval construings of knowledge and science to understand the new science, to generalize its ideas, and to adjust them to the inherited pattern of beliefs in other areas.

Or again, confronted by the overwhelming idea of Darwinian evolution, late nineteenth-century philosophers turned to one of the three major early nineteenth-century philosophical traditions, the Kantian, the Hegelian, or the empiricist and positivistic. They turned to these recognized philosophies of science to help them to come to terms with the novel idea, to assist them in exploring its implications, and in assimilating it to what they could understand, because they had always understood it that way. It is significant that it can be said, that the philosophical reaction to the idea of relativity, has so far been for a representative of each major tradition in our own world to demonstrate that relativity confirms the validity of his own inherited assumptions.

Men do not start their philosophizing by observing the world, or from "experience," unencumbered by ideas as to what the world, experience, and knowledge of them are. Not even the happy Greeks could do so. Our knowledge of the intellectual aspects of the Near Eastern cultures has already come to be sufficient for us to realize, what our previous ignorance kept us from knowing, that the Greeks began, not with looking at the world, but with criticizing the Mesopotamian cosmogonies of which their own religious tradition was but a variant. One of the few men in the history of thought to try consciously to turn away from the philosophy of the "schools"—the usual name for a philosophical tradition—to observe the world afresh and directly, was Bernardino Telesio. And he in fact turned from the physics of Aristotle to—the physics of Empedocles and of the Stoics. Francis Bacon called Telesio "the first of the moderns," *primus novorum virorum*, because he forsook Aristotle to observe the world.

But he also criticized Telesio severely, for observing the wrong things.

The major philosophical traditions that have figured during the history of Western philosophizing fall into several main groups. When Western Europe began its intellectual awakening, and looked to the ancient world for its schooling, it found four main philosophical traditions coming down from classic times: the Platonic, embodied for the West in the Augustinian writings, with an independent strain coming from Dionysius the Areopagite and John Scotus Eriugena; the Aristotelian, already embodied in the Arabic and the Jewish religious traditions, and available also in Sicily and in Constantinople in the late Greek form; the atomistic tradition, known principally through Lucretius; and the sceptical, to be found in Sextus Empiricus. Material from all these traditions was also available in the philosophical writings of Cicero, and in the more historical references of the patristic period, like those in the *City of God*. Perhaps, if Richard McKeon is right, we ought to recognize a fifth relatively independent tradition, the Ciceronian tradition of rhetoric, immensely influential during the Renaissance.

We have already enumerated the three major medieval traditions into which all this classical material was organized, and which were inherited by the seventeenth century. But already the characteristic national traditions of the modern period had begun to take form. Cartesianism, the heir of the rationalism of thirteenth-century Paris, has continued as the main current of thought in France, even when rebaptized in the Enlightenment in the name of Newton, and fertilized with Schelling by Victor Cousin under the Restoration. The empiricist tradition in England begins with William of Ockham in the fourteenth century. In the form familiar since the eighteenth century as "British," its grandfather is Hobbes and its two fathers Newton and Locke. The German tradition, an Augustinianism still more suffused with *Innerlichkeit*, begins with the fourteenth-century speculative mystics, Johann Tauler and Heinrich Suso, reaches developed form in fifteenth-century Nicholas of Cusa, and acquires its characteristic scientific and conceptual stamp in Leibniz. In the nineteenth century the German tradition split into three characteristic types, the Kantian, the Hegelian, and the *Lebensphilosophie* of the last three generations. Perhaps we can say that Peirce, James, and Dewey initiated a distinctively American philosophical tradition.

Each of these clusters of ideas exhibits certain characteristic and persisting assumptions: each has its own starting-point, approach, method, and concepts. Each has a type of problem it is best suited to deal with, and each confronts a set of intellectual difficulties peculiarly its own.

What is meant concretely by two different national traditions can be illustrated from the contrast between the two men who had the most influence in forming the intellectual traditions in England and in Germany, respectively, Newton and Leibniz. Newton's conception of knowledge was realistic: he was convinced he had discovered the structure of nature itself, "the plan by which the universe was made." Nature was a mathematical order, embodied in the masses which were "solid, massy, hard, impenetrable, movable particles," which acted on the human sensorium to produce the phenomena or sense-images from which its mathematical properties and structure could be "deduced." Newton was in fact surprisingly conservative in his view of what he called "the real world." He had made force and the calculus essential to his "natural philosophy" or scientific thought. But he quite failed to develop their implications when he came to sketch his world-view or "philosophy of nature." In that enterprise he simply took over the geometrical world already laid down by Galileo and Descartes: his own novel mathematical concepts made little difference.

In contrast, his contemporary Leibniz made force and calculus basic in his view of the world; in the light of what was to come in science, he seems to evince a much greater insight and profundity. Leibniz really thought in terms of the calculus, not of geometry and matter in motion, like Newton. He considered the latter's geometrical, Platonic world carefully, first in its Cartesian version, and toward the end, in his correspondence with Clarke, in its Newtonian form; and he rejected it as unintelligible.

Newton and Leibniz thus illustrate the difference between the British and the German intellectual traditions, in science as well as in philosophy. British thought since Newton—and since Locke, who made all the same Cartesian assumptions— has been dominated by the notion that knowledge is a matter of sense-images and their relations. Since Leibniz, for German thinking knowledge is rather an affair of equations and formulae. With the outstanding exception of Clerk Maxwell, the British scientist has been unhappy, like Humphry Davy, when he could not picture a world of substantial particles. The German has been satisfied with a world mathematically related in correlated functional series. The British thinker has not been content till he could picture a world he could imagine, on a visual model. The German has sought a world he could conceive as a mathematical system. To understand a phenomenon, like magnetism, the British have had to invent a mechanical model, like Faraday and Kelvin; they have often been held back by their refusal to admit what is unimaginable.

The empiricist tradition, in which the elements of knowledge are images and sensations, has proved almost ineradicable. The Germans have seen knowledge rather as a matter of *Begriffe* and *Verhältnisse*, of concepts and relations and systems of formulated laws—the whole set of terms familiar in the Kantian tradition, so close to the German tradition of natural science.

Today, it seems that the Newtonian world, the British tradition, is crumbling in science: the image, the very notion of substance, is disappearing from scientific thought. No mechanical model seems possible for the systems of radiation we now handle mathematically with such confidence. The physicists now present us with a world that is literally unimaginable—to the layman, though hardly to the mathematician, it often seems unintelligible as well. Leibniz is triumphant, Newton is beaten. Planck and Einstein have vanquished Oliver Lodge, and Heisenberg and Schrödinger, Niels Bohr, British in his thinking. In the early twenties there used to be on display in departments of physics mechanical models of the "Bohr atom." They have since been quietly removed. But we do not need to dilate here on the relative fertility of these two national traditions; it is enough to use them to illustrate what a national intellectual tradition is. One might add Bertrand Russell's observation, that American rats, placed in mazes, dash around madly and finally by accident blunder out; while in the same mazes German rats sit down quietly, figure out the exit, and proceed sedately to it. Even rats have a national tradition—in the laboratories of psychologists.

It has been more and more borne in upon me, that it is these philosophical traditions that are the fundamental units in the history of philosophy. The isolated unit-ideas of Arthur O.

Lovejoy's very atomistic conception of intellectual history have always seemed inadequate to historians with a sense of how long-continued are the interrelations between certain ideas. But so long as the only alternative seemed to be a denial of analysis, the contention that each philosophy is an indivisible, unanalyzable, "organic" whole, they have hesitated to brave Mr. Lovejoy's just wrath. But here, in these clusters of related assumptions and concepts, we seem to find genuine units, strands that can be clearly distinguished from other strands often interwoven with them, and that can themselves be picked apart into their component threads. The intellectual unit is not an atomic idea, it is a system—an "organic" system, not in the sense that it cannot be analyzed, but in the sense that it is growing and living, responding to the countless pressures that impinge on it from other sources.

To vary the figure, such a philosophical tradition is a kind of toolbox, a set of instruments a philosopher has at his disposal, in working on his own problems. Or it is like a language, developed to express certain aspects of the world that have vitally impressed the original statesman-philosopher who put it together and launched it on its career. Each cluster of assumptions has its own distinctive advantages: it was worked out originally to deal with certain problems, and to emphasize certain features of the world and life and knowledge. Each has the job it can do best. But by the same mark, each tradition has its own particular difficulties, problems it finds it peculiarly hard to deal with. And each has its characteristic dangers and pitfalls, impasses and blind alleys into which it can lead thought if they be not foreseen in time.

Now, it is precisely the history of a tradition that best reveals what it can and what it cannot fruitfully accomplish. It is its history that illuminates its powers, and its limitations, the intellectual jobs it can tackle with promise of success, the problems it has never been able to do justice to, no matter how hard men have wrestled with the intractable instrument. It is its history that reveals how it needed reconstruction, modification through other ideas, when it confronted a novel problem.

Thus in the Middle Ages, the Christian Platonism of the Augustinian tradition could receive endless fruitful elaboration when applied to the intellectual problems of the soul and of God, for which Augustine had designed his instrument. But it had little of value to say about nature; and when the Schoolmen grew eager to explore the scene of human life, it drove them to turn rather to Aristotle, who had built his philosophy around nature and its categories. The atomistic tradition, when men turned to it in Rome, could convey and express for a Lucretius a majestic vision of nature's aspect and her law, and it could liberate alike from the passions of the love of woman and the fear of death, from the religion that can persuade to do so much of evil. It could still perform well the same function for a Santayana in the twentieth century. But it has never been able to treat the subtle intellectual problems that arise in the spiritual life of man. For them, men have normally turned to some variant of the inimitable and inexhaustible Platonic tradition.

No wonder Kant proved popular, and emancipating, when he combined the mathematical vision of the Platonic tradition with the experimental acknowledgement of fact of the Aristotelian, in a new cluster, a new form, that could dominate most nineteenth-century philosophy of natural science. The Kantian philosophy of science was a consummately skillful analysis of the scheme of intelligibility worked out in Newtonian science, an acute tabulation of its assumptions and intellectual methods, that for the first time in the century since Spinoza and Leibniz could give an intelligible construing of the fact of science and its now obvious success. Then the Kantian philosophy of mathematics encountered in the mid-nineteenth century the new fact of non-Euclidean geometry, which drove it to a reconstruction and expansion of its original scheme of intelligibility. This earlier encounter prepared it to meet the necessary loosening of its rigid structure of understanding, forced on it by the fact of the twentieth-century revolution in physical theory—by the new, post-Newtonian conception of causality in quantum mechanics, for example.

The Kantian tradition considers science as an interpretation of the facts of observation in terms of a scheme of understanding. The major intellectual problem it has repeatedly faced has been the need of loosening up and rendering more flexible Kant's own scheme of interpretation and understanding, limited in Kant's horizon to the scheme consecrated in Newtonian thought, which Kant, like Newton himself, took as ultimate and final. The problem has been to realize that in our own scientific enterprise that scheme—what Kant called "pure reason"—with a growing body of science has had and continues to have a history. That is why the Neo-Kantians were led in the last generation to write their imposing histories of pure reason—Ernst Cassirer in his *Erkenntnisproblem*, and Léon Brunschvicg in his *Les Étapes de la philosophie mathématique*, and his *La Causalité et l'expérience humaine*.

The other major problem of the Kantian tradition has been to break down the sharp and unreal distinction Kant made between the assumptions of observation—the "forms of sense-intuition," which he took as psychological—and the assumptions of interpretation—the "categories of the understanding," which he made logical—the gulf between the "transcendental aesthetic" and the "transcendental analytic." This taking of observation as just given, as psychologically conditioned data, seems to have come for Kant himself from his being too much of a Lockean, from his having read too many Lockean analyses, especially that of Tetens. Whatever its other limitations, it is the achievement of the Marburg School of Neo-Kantians —of Hermann Cohen, Paul Natorp, and Ernst Cassirer—to effect that breakdown, and make all the assumptions logical. Thus the history of the Neo-Kantian tradition is an excellent illustration of the way a philosophical tradition grows and expands, and is provoked by new problems—non-Euclidean geometry, relativity of measurement, new concepts of causality—to successful self-criticism.

If the major problem of the Kantian tradition has been to get rid of the rigidity of its scheme of interpretation, the major problem of the empiricist tradition has always been to provide some place for the schemes of interpretation scientists actually employ. That empirical philosophy of science, as we find it in Newton and Locke as a kind of second best, forced upon them by their inability to make intelligible on Ockhamite assumptions the earlier rationalistic conception of science, and as we find it consistently set forth in Berkeley as the structure of human knowledge, runs: science is the description in mathematical formulation of the observed course of nature. But scientists do more than describe, they interpret and organize, and the problem of the empiricists has always been to provide an intelligible account of that interpretation and organization, and its intellectual instruments. So long as much science itself remained thus descriptive and empirical, like the botany of Linnaeus, and employed merely what Stuart Mill called "descriptive generalizations" or hypotheses, the empirical account of science could seem plausible and adequate. But with the rise of a genuinely experimental science —a hypothetical-deductive experimental science, to give it a more accurate characterization—empiricists confronted the problem of finding a place for the role of explanatory and causal hypotheses. The problem became increasingly acute as science came to employ the wealth of hypothesis and of theoretical construction we are familiar with today. At this point the empiricist tradition had to seize on mathematical logic with its wealth of calculi, to provide their account with a scheme of interpretation in mathematical language. In logical empiricism the empiricist tradition has approached the expanded Neo-Kantian philosophy. It can be said, in fact, that logical empiricism is both a reconstructed empiricist philosophy, and the form the Kantian philosophy has come to assume today, with the categories of a freely manipulable symbolic logic replacing those of a now antiquated "pure reason." It is the Kantian philosophy purified of its remnant of Lockean psychologism and given logical consistency by means of present-day techniques.

Here are two cardinal examples of the historical working-out of two important philosophical traditions, typical patterns of the kind of historical change we encounter. In all but terminology, the two traditions have tended to converge—an historical pattern we must shortly consider. No Kantian can now work in his tradition, no empiricist can labor in his, without being aware of these patterns of reconstruction and enlargement. Indeed, it is difficult to conceive any philosopher working in an intellectual tradition—as he must—and using that tradition today, without being historically aware of how his cluster of assumptions has taken the form in which it has come into his hands. He must know the history, the strong points, the besetting dangers and pitfalls, of the intellectual

language, the approach, methods, concepts, and goals, he
elects, or is by his education compelled, to use.

There are other types of pattern also that force themselves
on the attention of the student of the history of philosophical
traditions. Thus there is a general pattern to be observed in
the working out of such a tradition, from an initial confidence
in the power of man's reason to answer all the questions it can
raise, to the gradual realization that while reason can pose
questions, in the last analysis it is unable to answer any of them
in the way it had originally hoped. This is one of the broad
patterns of intellectual movements, illustrated again and again
with many a variation in detail. As so often in the history of
our Western culture, the classic illustration occurs in the
development of medieval thinking. Medieval philosophizing
began, with John Scotus Eriugena in the ninth century, and
again with Anselm in the eleventh, in a confident Christian
Platonism that reaches its high point in the thought of those
rational mystics, Hugh and Richard of St. Victor, in the early
twelfth century. All these Augustinian Platonists, knowing
only one intellectual tradition, which had descended to them
in direct line from the ancient world, and serenely unaware
of any conflicting interpretations of the world and experience
of it, were convinced that every question could be solved.
Anselm's attitude is well illustrated in the title of his major
theological treatise, *Cur Deus Homo? Why did God become
man?* The fact is accepted on faith; understanding and reason
can supply the explanation. It was the Victorine Richard who
answered more questions than any other medieval thinker,
possibly than any other in the Western tradition. He gave
the perfect rationalization, as we have come to say, of all the
doctrines of faith.

Then Aristotle was discovered, and his intellectual power led men to take him as the model of what reason could accomplish unaided. But lo! Aristotle's natural reason was quite unable, on its own principles, to prove the characteristic doctrines of the faith. They lay beyond what was now carefully distinguished, first by Thomas, and then more narrowly by Duns Scotus, as the province within which reason is valid. Reason is not omnicompetent, it is definitely limited in scope. William of Ockham appears, and reason continues to shrink. It can now establish of itself nothing about existence; for that we must go to experience alone. Reason can ascertain only the identity of terms. Not even the first table of the Decalogue, which Duns Scotus had left within the competence of reason to establish, can be so supported. The will of God is a sheer empirical fact, to be established by revelation alone—or by observing things as they are. Finally, John of Mirecourt and Nicholas of Autrecourt, in the next generation, destroy the possibility of rational inference from present observation to the future, or even—granting the power of God at any moment to perform a miracle—of inference from phantasmata to their natural causes. Reason, so supreme in the twelfth century, has been by the fourteenth shut out of the world and locked up in the dialectic of terms.

With the seventeenth century, reason returned triumphant in mathematics. In Descartes, in Spinoza, in Leibniz and the other proud rationalists, mathematical reason was once more supreme legislator. But Newton was stopped by the undiscoverable "force" of gravitation, and in Hume reason had shrunk once more to the modest realm of the relations between ideas based on similarity. And James Mill reduced similarity itself to mere encountered contiguity: reason was the purely given or accidental association of ideas. Even Kant had to accept the nub of Hume's criticism: reason of itself could establish nothing about existence where it could not found itself on observation, it could operate only in the realm of possible experience.

Once more reason returned—now, not the "abstract reason" of the dogmatic rationalists, but the "concrete" historical reason of Hegel. Now at last men had discovered an intellectual instrument which could really explain why everything is as it is and why it must be so. That reason is still enthroned beyond the iron curtain. But in our Western lands, where reason has been most free to work out its destiny, even Hegel's concrete reason, it grew, in an F. H. Bradley or a John Dewey, into the tool of a pluralistic, objective, functional relativism. In everything but the formulation of an ultimate intellectual ideal, for Bradley the end is a devastating scepticism; and for Dewey, reason does not even bother with "pure truth."

Thus the pattern of an intellectual movement, as illustrated by scholasticism, by the mathematical rationalism of the seventeenth century, and by the Hegelian tradition alike, seems to be from confidence to scepticism. The discovery of a new intellectual instrument provokes high hopes, especially when no other is known, or when the discredited rival has been discarded. Then the process of self-criticism begins, stimulated by the impact of other ideas which that instrument is not prepared to handle. The outcome leaves men groping for a new instrument of reason.

Our own century has seen the same process once more. Bertrand Russell, in his quest for certainty, was at first convinced that the new techniques of mathematical logic could solve all the problems. They could establish the foundation of mathematics, including mathematical induction. They could even solve the problem of empirical induction, which Hume had left as central; they could create a language in which everything could be said exactly with perfect precision. But the hopes faded. Logical atomism could not find the perfect language, induction could not be transformed into a deductive postulate system. The quest for certainty had failed.* Russell is left the intellectual sceptic: only as a poet and a moralist has he found certainty. In his own liftetime Wittgenstein went through the same disillusionment. But he came out with a faith in the power of linguistic analysis. Is it any wonder, however, that the student, familiar with this pattern of human thinking from confidence to humility, still retains doubts as to whether, by the new techniques of clearing up the muddles caused by the faulty use of language, we can solve in a generation all the soluble philosophical problems, and easily dispose of all the others?

Nor is this pattern of the historical development of an intellectual movement based on the initial faith in certain instruments of reason, something confined to our Western culture since the Middle Ages. In ancient thought, the course of Platonism is the real classic example. Taken as a philosophy of human life, the Platonic tradition, starting with Plato's own vision of the Good, as something as certain as mathematics, and attainable by the same "dialectical" reasoning, reached its outcome in the scepticism of Arcesilaos and Carneades, the "Academic philosophy" of Cicero, and of Hume. Platonism as a religious philosophy, which we take as initiated by the greatest of the Greek rationalists, Plotinos, and as transmitted to the West through Augustine's answer to the sceptics, reaches its end in the humanized Augustinian

* See Russell's *Human Knowledge* (New York, Simon and Schuster, 1948); and for the pattern of the movement in general, J. O. Urmson's *Philosophical Analysis* (Oxford, 1956).

scepticism of a Gerson, a Montaigne, or a Pascal. Platonism as a mathematical philosophy of nature, so self-satisfied in Descartes, least sceptical of thinkers, led in a generation to the scepticism of any rational science of nature in a Malebranche —so controlling over Hume's thinking—and to the scepticism of any knowledge of human nature, of man's "essence," as the existentialists say, in Pascal.

Let us look more closely at this pattern of the criticism and reconstruction of the assumptions of a single tradition. British empiricism is an excellent illustration. For in each generation this cluster of ideas has produced an acute analyst and critic, honest enough to recognize the limitations of his assumptions, and intelligent enough to push on to others. These major empiricist philosophers start always with one set of assumptions, inherited from their predecessors; they start with one conception of the nature of science and of its status, and they uniformly emerge with another. Locke set out with the Cartesian ideal of science; he was led to so much that was "plainly fact, but incomprehensible," that he emerged with the descriptive or observational theory of science. Hume started with this observationalism, and came out with a form of experimentalism. Stuart Mill, starting with father's observationalism, likewise transformed it into experimentalism—the "deductive method," he called his variety. Whitehead sets out with the Lockean views of Russell, and emerges with a radical empiricism and an experimentalism.

Let us consider the major assumptions of empiricism, as they appear in Locke. We can list them as:

1. Science is not "certain": it is not demonstrative, but is merely descriptive of the observed course of events. This conception of science we are calling "observationalism."

2. Science is not of the world, but of the effects of the world on the mind: it is of the contents of the mind. This view is called "subjectivism," though a more accurate term would be Hume's "double existence hypothesis."

3. In knowing, the mind is completely passive: it does nothing itself but receive impressions. This view James called the "spectator theory" of knowledge. This is not completely Locke's own assumption, but his active principle of "reflection" was soon turned into passivity in Condillac and in James Mill.

4. The original of knowledge is the criterion of its extent and certainty; its validity is determined by "how the mind comes to be furnished with ideas," and is tested by the "impressions from which they are derived," by the "data of experience." This is the genetic criterion of the validity of knowledge.

Of these four cardinal assumptions of the empiricist tradition, the first, the observational conception of science, was first made consistent by Berkeley. He transformed all the inherent and nonrelational concepts still left in Newton and Locke into relational and therefore observable concepts, and set forth what we can call a "relational realism"—the modern term is "objective relativism." For him, Newton's troublesome nonrelational "forces," Locke's inherent "powers," are gone—those assumptions Berkeley transformed. Berkeley did indeed retain the notion of nonrelational "powers" in two places, in the notions of the self and of God.

Hume got rid of both, making the self wholly relational, and denying rational status to God. Hume also transformed Locke's and Berkeley's observationalism into an experimental conception of science, taking science ultimately as the experimental confirmation of hypotheses or assumptions. With this experimentalism of Hume's Kant agreed, and elaborated it on a large scale. Kant is the first major theorist of an experimental science, after the Dutch Newtonians s'Gravesande and Musschenbroek. Stuart Mill went through the same process of self-criticism once more, likewise transforming observationalism into experimentalism.

The second assumption of empiricism, the subjectivism which raised for Locke the problem of the "reality" of knowledge, Berkeley categorically denies. That knowledge is in Locke's sense "real," is his starting point. Hume showed that this subjectivistic assumption is really meaningless, since it makes no discernible difference—at least at those times when he is not adopting it for his own malicious and critical purposes. Subjectivism was transformed by William James, in abolishing the Cartesian notion of "consciousness." Following Renouvier, he arrived at his "radical empiricism," which meant also that relations as well as terms are given in experience. Hume likewise emerged with a similar radical empiricism, deriving relations from a "habit of mind" or the "imagination." Kant derived them from "pure reason"; the logical positivists derive them from logical calculi; the followers of Wittgenstein, from the categories of language. Stuart Mill and Whitehead have given central emphasis to the rejection of the assumption of subjectivism. Hume's "double existence hypothesis" Whitehead calls the fallacy of the "bifurcation of nature" into a causal nature and a perceived nature.

These first two assumptions of the empiricist tradition, observationalism and subjectivism, are what we have called its more superficial assumptions: they have been overcome and rejected again and again. But the remaining two assumptions are more deep-seated, and much harder to get rid of. The way to escape the spectator theory of knowledge, or the complete passivity of the mind in knowing, is to transform it into a more active conception, in which knowledge is taken as involving an activity of the thinker as well as the reception of "data." This really begins in Hume, who finds ideas associated by a "gentle force." But it is made central in Kant's "Copernican" view of knowledge as an active interpretation of observations. How persistent is the spectator theory is clear in Whitehead's long struggle to emancipate himself from it.

The fourth assumption, the genetic criterion of the validity of knowledge, is likewise extremely difficult to overcome. Hume's analysis of the various major ideas of our intellectual life really destroyed it once and for all. He showed it is impossible to distinguish a "sound" and "solid system" of ideas from an unsound system on the basis of which impressions it is derived from, for both are derived from the same impressions. But he did not state this conclusion explicitly, and it remained for Kant to work his way out of Locke's geneticism into the alternative, a functional test of validity. The first critique leaves the categories or principles of interpretation "pure," that is, without any function, save to "constitute" science. But in the third critique, they become "regulative" and genuinely functional.

The voluntarists of the next generation, in a Fichte, for instance, made pure reason the servant of practical reason, and thus gave it the function of serving man's moral will. But it was the biological conception of human nature and of knowing, stimulated by Darwin, that reinforced this voluntaristic functionalism, and led to the pragmatic functionalism of a Nietzsche, a James, and a Bergson; just as it was biology that gave scientific standing to Hegel's social functionalism, in a George Herbert Mead and a John Dewey. But on the whole, it has been the voluntarism of the recent German tradition that since Kant and Hegel has explored an active and functional conception of man's knowing process. The main British tradition, since it forgot Bradley's functionalism, has persisted in the two most deep-seated assumptions of the empiricist cluster of ideas. It is the Americans who have emphasized the biological construing of the Kantian and the Hegelian types of functionalism.*

One further point might be added. In this self-criticism of a philosophical tradition, the final analysis and reconstruction is usually the work of a thinker who by some special combination of circumstances is relatively disinterested, freed from the drive to solve a practical problem of adjustment. Such practical interests normally do not control the direction a thinker takes, so much as the point at which he will stop short, when he has arrived at an idea that will serve his purposes, instead of pushing his analysis and criticism to the very end. Such disinterested analysis is able to follow out the implications of assumptions wherever they may lead. Thus Spinoza could explore the full consequences of denying teleology and potentiality. Berkeley was held back when he arrived at the notion of spiritual power. His episcopal status did not drive him to his relational realism, which actually delayed his preferment for years: he seemed far too erratic even for an Irish bishop. But it did prevent him from taking

---

* For the historical details and justification of this brief account of the fortunes of the British tradition of empiricism, see the author's *Career of Philosophy: From the Middle Ages to the Enlightenment* (New York, Columbia University Press, 1962). The relevant analyses are in Book IV.

the final steps which Hume's lack of real interest in science permitted him. By a different set of circumstances, Bradley was another such disinterested thinker.

This power of self-criticism exhibited by a philosophical tradition, by an associated cluster of assumptions, points to another historical pattern repeatedly illustrated, the tendency of rival philosophical traditions to converge as they work themselves out, when their assumptions are elaborated and criticized with honesty, and in the light of all the facts. Hence the particular starting point, the particular philosophical tradition that one begins by accepting, with its own distinctive assumptions, in the end seems to be of little ultimate moment, and to be irrelevant—save for purely pedagogical purposes, and for bringing to light the reasons for the limitations found in every actual philosophical analysis. Each traditional cluster of ideas has its own advantages and conveniences: it can more easily deal with those traits and distinctions it is led to emphasize. Likewise, each cluster displays its own specific neglects, the traits it is likely to minimize or to overlook. Each has its own pitfalls into which it is prone to plunge. And each bears the scars of the particular battles it has waged, its own distinctive emphases and loaded terms, of praise and disparagement, its own pet antipathies and abominations.

But history shows, that from their various starting-points, each in his own tradition, men have been led, by the same permanences of their experience of a common world, to recognize and formulate, each in his own particular philosophical language, certain common distinctions and traits— common, because they are translatable into counterparts in all the other philosophical languages. They are different ways of stating the fundamental pattern of what is, and of how it is to be understood.

These different philosophical languages—the language of experience, the language of being, the languages of the various particular traditions—of Plato, of Aristotle, of Kant, of the empiricists, of the experientialists—are after all each talking of the same world. And if they be carried far enough, they are all forced by man's universal experience of that common world to make the same distinctions. The different philosophical traditions, in their development, as they work out the implications of their respective assumptions, and are used to deal with the same particular problems of an age, come in the end to the same distinctions: they come to recognize the same truths about the world men encounter, the same pervasive traits.

Historically, the starting point of philosophic activity has consisted in criticism of particular views inherited, carried on in terms of certain distinctive assumptions. But the peculiar assumptions chosen—or inherited—as initial instruments of criticism, seem in the long run to make no major difference, if they be worked with, honestly and open-mindedly, to take account of all the facts to which they direct men, and to which other assumptions lead them, if elaborated and pushed where they point, and if modified in the process of use to do justice to what is discovered, if their inadequacies be remedied. Philosophical differences remain just because this honest process of enlarging and reconstructing is never in fact carried through to "ultimately."

Any system or body of beliefs is the expression and formulation of certain relations selected from the experienced world, in a definite intellectual language, with a vocabulary and grammar of its own. The expression and formulation always has a history, of development and modification, as men learn to face new problems, and old ones in novel con-

texts. Men can even change their philosophical language pretty drastically, if their interest in knowing shifts profoundly, as it did in the seventeenth century. They can enlarge and expurgate their vocabulary, and extend and modify their grammar, in the interest of the more adequate expression of the new subject-matter they have come to be interested in, like matter in motion in Galileo's day.

The Western philosophical tradition, though expressed always in different languages, has still revealed a common pattern of what is and how to understand it. This pattern has been forced upon thinkers by efforts to express the same facts, the same structure of a common world. That Western tradition began with a common heritage, Greek thought, to which it has again and again returned for fresh insight. In all its separate traditions, it has been held together, or brought together again, when divergences have developed, by the same natural science, encountered in successive waves. Rival interpretations of the same new scientific idea, when followed out searchingly and honestly for several generations, have again and again tended to converge. It is new problems presented by an altered social experience that have normally caused the splitting up into rival parties and philosophies once again. But then these philosophies, built around divergent social values, have again and again been brought together once more by the challenge of a new scientific idea. Social experience has usually fostered divergencies; it is science that has been the unifying factor in the intellectual life of the West, setting limits that cannot be disregarded, and forcing common directions that must be followed.

Thus we see the convergence of these various traditions, a convergence that seems to be historically emergent, a convergence toward a common metaphysics. The particular philosophical language in which it is expressed becomes less and less of a barrier. For the different philosophical languages —the languages of the different philosophical traditions—seem to be approaching the point where they are ultimately translatable into each other's terms—perhaps in the end into a common tongue. It is of the utmost importance to know several at least of these different philosophical languages, and what they have historically been saying—indeed, as many as one may. For only thus is it possible to distinguish in what they are saying between what is mere grammar and vocabulary, and what is genuine subject-matter. What is in each in the end not translatable, is pretty sure to be bound up with the accidental forms and structure of a particular language, and not the expression of what is inherent in the subject-matter, in the "evident situation," in human life in its natural setting and its human vision.

III. How History Brings Philosophical Understanding

In the previous chapter, we have given a number of instances of various types of historical pattern that can be found by examining the philosophical record of our Western culture. We have done so, in the hope, in part at least, that these concrete illustrations of historical relations between philosophical ideas and philosophical traditions would reveal something of the kind of illumination that can come from approaching philosophical materials historically. In this chapter, we shall go on to examine and analyze in greater detail, just what kinds of illumination historical knowledge does contribute to philosophical, as contrasted with purely historical, understanding.

For we may well agree, that intellectual history is a fascinating pursuit. It reveals to us men thinking, and something of how their minds are operating when they are thinking. The historical treatment of philosophy, it is clear, illuminates all the other strands of cultural history. Conceived as it has been here portrayed, as the intellectual reaction of outstanding minds to other cultural and culturally significant events, it displays not merely ideas in the process of being worked out. It displays ideas in action, as they intervene in the other activities of men, and influence the course of institutional development. It thus helps us to understand ourselves, and our culture, our intellectual world. It throws light on why we find the ideas we find that control our thinking, and that offer opportunities to us to think further by using them. The history of philosophical ideas thus helps to make clear what our available ideas are. It does this in part, but only in part. For what the history of our ideas illuminates is what our ideas *have been*, and what they have been able so far to do—what men have been able to accomplish by employing them. But it does not, and cannot, tell us what those ideas *can* do, what we can hope to achieve by using and perhaps reconstructing them. For that does not depend on their past, that depends on us, on what we have the wit to attempt and the ability to carry through. It depends on what we discover we can do with them. Thus we can say that history reveals much, but teaches nothing. It reveals what has been, and illuminates what is. But it does not teach us what will be.*

We may grant that the history of philosophy contributes much to our understanding of many things in our culture. But we can still ask—and many students of philosophy are asking today—what has this history of our predecessors to do with our own philosophizing? They had their own problems— granted! But we have ours—and they are very different. They had their own intellectual methods. But we have found better ones. Why, then, should we not employ our up-to-date methods on our own philosophical problems, and forget the irrelevant past? Why not use the powerful new techniques we have now elaborated—symbolic logic, categorial analysis, or whatever seems to us to offer promise—to settle whatever

* For a fuller analysis of what historical knowledge contributes to the understanding of the present, and for the theme of this chapter in general, see the author's *Nature and Historical Experience* (New York: Columbia University Press, 1958), Part I, "Towards a Theory of History," chapter 4 and especially 5.

problems may be left over from the past, once and for all, and then go on to new questions?

Why should we not learn from the procedure of science, and take that successful procedure as our model? The practice of scientific inquiry is notoriously not its history. Is it not the case equally that the practice of philosophy is not its history? Let us be interested as much as we will in the past, for its own sake and its own fascination. But let us not fool ourselves. When we begin to philosophize on our own, we must resolutely turn our backs on the past and tackle our intellectual problems afresh, and directly.

This program sounds attractive, and has come to awaken wide acceptance among students of philosophy today, especially in English-speaking countries. For one thing, it relieves them of so much intellectual responsibility for a knowledge which to be significant has to be pursued painstakingly and with much labor. And much of the policy it advocates is indeed sound. We should, of course, be prepared to tackle the intellectual problems of our own day, not merely those of the past. We certainly should employ the best methods we have found, with all the new ideas we can discover or imagine.

But it may be significant, that most of those who are most loudly proclaiming a new intellectual method today, are not using it to deal with fresh problems, with the problems of the underlying intellectual conflicts and tensions in our own culture today. They seem rather to be applying their new philosophical method to inherited problems and conflicts and muddles. They seem to be using it, not to arrive at constructive working solutions of the intellectual difficulties that insistently confront us, but rather to make clear that previous thinkers came to the wrong answers and formulated the wrong conclusions. They tell us they are devoted to the therapeutic attempt to clear up the muddles of the past, and cure us from anxiety about them. They scorn the responsibility of the challenging attempt to clarify and guide the future.

One begins to suspect, that the resolve to turn our backs on the past as irrelevant, and to approach things afresh with our new techniques, is apt to lead us to an entangled concern with problems inherited from the past, that are irrelevant to the intellectual issues of today. It is apt to lead to the more precise elaboration of unquestioned inherited assumptions, that can only distort those present intellectual issues. So one begins to wonder, whether to forget the past, and follow the procedure of the model of science, is not to be led to a philosophy that is academic and scholastic, and has lost any real function in the intellectual life of today.

Now surely, to concern ourselves exclusively with past philosophers and their problems, to identify the pursuit of philosophy with the study of its history, is to abandon the philosophic enterprise. There was indeed much in the academic philosophizing of the late nineteenth century, and in the epigonic cultivation of the Hegelian tradition when it had lost its original promise and stimulus, that helps to explain the disgusted reaction of our own generation. They tell us this had much to do with the revulsion of French students of philosophy against the too-exclusive preoccupation of French university teaching with the study of the intellectual tradition, when those students were presented with a real crisis in 1940, and felt the urge to act, and think about action.

But equally, one begins to suspect, as one observes present-day attempts at a philosophizing wholly liberated from much knowledge of the past, to fail to learn how to use the past of philosophy is to repeat the errors and the follies of that past.

To use history is the only alternative to remaining its slave. To escape a continuing bondage to the past, we must understand the past. Only thus can we make it our servant and instrument, and not leave it our master. For the past will be one or the other. The past is what we must work with. It is what has given us our ideas, our categories, our assumptions, our methods, our techniques, the procedures available to bring to bear on our problems. Our entire stock of intellectual resources is inescapably a heritage from the past: it is embodied history itself, the past alive in the present. This past is a human achievement, the deposit of man's long intellectual wrestling with his world. It is an achievement, but an imperfect achievement. It is limited, selective, one-sided, incomplete, and distorting. It includes, to be sure, fertile ideas, methods of great promise, assumptions that have shown their power to lead to fruitful results. But it also embraces mistakes, false paths that lead nowhere, *Holzwege*, misleading distinctions, assumptions that have led again and again to blocked impasses, models that have turned out to be barren. Only through the understanding that history brings can we discriminate what we may hope to use fruitfully in our own philosophizing, from what we had best discard. It is not only the analysis of language that can prove emancipating and therapeutic. Historical knowledge is the greatest of all liberators from the mistakes and muddles, from the tyranny of the past.

Why, then, cannot the philosopher like the scientist disregard the history of the ideas he finds useful, and start from the present state of philosophical achievement, from where we are now? Why is it not enough for the philosopher, like the scientist, to plunge *in medias res*? Now, the model of the scientific enterprise is itself pretty tricky, and not always adequately understood by the scientist himself. That is one reason why it is always necessary for the philosopher to be interpreting the scientist's changing enterprise to the scientist himself, not merely to the layman. What has emerged as a central philosophical discipline today, the philosophy of science, is not mere vulgarization for the uninitiated of what every scientist knows. It is rather a holding up of the mirror to the scientist himself—still better, the focusing of a lens upon him and his activities, that will produce a clearer and more distinct image of what he is doing, usually without much self-awareness on his own part. The scientific model appealed to by philosophers today is tricky, because while there are marked resemblances between the enterprise of the scientist and of the philosopher, there are equally basic differences. It is necessary to be clear about both.

In the first place, the scientist does not start *de novo*. His failure to get further in the ancient world, despite his brilliant ideas, is primarily due to the lack of cumulative continuity in scientific thinking in that age. Only when science had become institutionalized in the Italian universities did it begin to make what we can call "steady progress." The scientist, in point of fact, always starts, like the philosopher, from a funded body of ideas. He starts as the heir of the results and achievements of a cumulative enterprise with a long past of previous inquiry behind it. Aristotle knew that, and illustrates it himself. But it was after him soon forgotten, save by the mathematicians and astronomers. The scientist never makes a completely "fresh start." If the philosopher is indeed anxious to follow the model of the scientist, he would do well to abandon the mantle of the prophet, proclaiming each day a fresh new revelation—a mantle he has worn only too often, especially in Germany, since the Romanticists elevated the prophetic function of philosophy. He would do well to follow rather the cumulative and cooperative procedure of the scientist. The philosopher, like the scientist, should "know his field" before he begins innovating. Men like Morris Cohen and Arthur Lovejoy used to preach that lesson unceasingly. And it has been objected against Dewey, with some justice, that he always conducted his fresh inquiries in a kind of historical museum: like Aristotle, he always began his consideration of any problem with a survey of his predecessors.

Secondly, there is actually much in the philosophic enterprise, as in science, that is cumulative and achieved. This is especially true of intellectual methods, which is why the history of philosophy has to make the elaboration of such methods the central strand in its interpretation. There are also concepts and distinctions which, once won, have proved of value ever after. There are classic criticisms of certain assumptions and certain arguments, with which any thinker today must come to terms; he can disregard them only at his peril. It was his almost total lack of interest in and ignorance of his "field," in this sense, that made the insights of Wittgenstein so much less fruitful than they might otherwise have been. It is this ignorance that is responsible for the cavalier disregard by many of his followers of the past, and of those willing to use it.

But, thirdly, the philosophic enterprise is not just like science. It is not the often erratic but on the whole fairly steady acquisition of new knowledge. It is fundamentally a process of criticism, ever renewed, of the ideas men are using, in the interest of meeting novel intellectual problems. And in such criticism, philosophers cannot with impunity make a completely "fresh start." Rather, to make their start effective, they often, indeed usually, have to go back to the "beginning," to examine just where the incompleteness or inadequacy of an idea came from, and how to modify it.

Hence, fourthly, while there is in philosophy an accumulated heritage that must be taken into consideration, there is not, as in science, any wholly accepted body of achieved and received ideas. There is rather a plurality of such bodies, grouped in the different philosophical traditions we were trying to delineate. There are various sets or clusters of assumptions and concepts that are indeed unquestioned, but are far from unquestionable. From this store each philosopher has to make his own selection. Even when he is impelled—and it is never a free choice or election—to work within one tradition, to be anything more than an epigone or "academic," the philosopher has to consider the other traditions and the illumination they offer, the utility they promise.

No major philosophical idea, unlike what holds of the older theories in science, is ever wholly "superseded." Atomism, or evolution, which first occurred to inquiring Greek minds, may be long forgotten. But in the face of a new intellectual situation, they can suddenly display their intellectual power. The Greeks, indeed, are as living as ever. No contemporary analysis of the language of ethics can afford not to begin with Aristotle; and no despiser of the past can avoid reckoning with Plato. Most of my historical illustrations have been drawn from medieval and modern philosophizing, and not from the Greeks, not because the Greeks are unimportant, but because it is so difficult to take them as belonging to "history." Plato and Aristotle, and the Stoics and Epicureans, are our intellectual contemporaries. They are companions and teachers in the present-day philosophical situation, as they always have been.

Alan Wood, author of a biography of Bertrand Russell, *The Passionate Skeptic*, writes in an introduction to an unfinished study of Russell's philosophy printed in Russell's own *My Philosophical Development*:

Russell did not acquire much knowledge of philosophy—in the usual academic sense of studying the writings of other philosophers—until comparatively late in life. He did not read philosophy officially until his fourth year at Cambridge, and his course of study at Cambridge had some important gaps. As a boy, Russell arrived at something like Descartian dualism before he read Descartes; he had Humean doubts before he read Hume. I am inclined to think that his lack of systematic philosophical education was an advantage, and that nothing can do more to stultify original thinking than a thorough knowledge of past philosophers acquired too early in life; because it brings with it the deadening discouragement of realizing that most of the ideas one thinks up have been thought of by someone else before. (Perhaps the classic example of the advantages of ignorance was Wittgenstein.)*

Whatever his biographer may have thought, Russell himself hardly shares that opinion. In his recent *Wisdom of the West* he writes:

The current trend towards more and fiercer specialisms is making men forget their intellectual debts to their forbears. This study aims to counter such forgetfulness. In some serious sense, all Western philosophy is Greek philosophy; and it is idle to indulge in philosophic thought while cutting the ties that link us with the great thinkers of the past. It used once to be held, perhaps wrongly, that it was meet for a philosopher to know something

* Alan Wood, "Russell's Philosophy," in Bertrand Russell, *My Philosophical Development* (New York: Simon and Schuster, 1959), p. 274.

about everything. Philosophy claimed all knowledge for its province. However this may be, the prevailing view that philosophers need know nothing about anything is quite certainly wrong. Those who think that philosophy "really" began in 1921, or at any rate not long before, fail to see that current philosophic problems have not arisen all of a sudden and out of nothing. No apology is therefore offered for the comparatively generous treatment of Greek philosophy. . . .

In some vital respects the philosophic tradition of the West differs from the speculations of the Eastern mind. There is no civilization but the Greek in which a philosophic movement goes hand in hand with a scientific tradition. It is this that gives the Greek enterprise its peculiar scope; it is this dual tradition that has shaped the civilization of the West.*

In one respect Russell's vigorous statement needs supplementing. The current disparaging of the history of philosophy in England is not due merely to philosophy's having become highly technical—to what Russell calls its "fierce specialism." It is due also to the natural reaction against the dominance in academic circles for almost two generations of the teaching of the Hegelian philosophy, with its central claim that present philosophizing—meaning Hegel's—is the culmination of the whole philosophical development of the Western tradition. Hegel viewed that development as a unilinear "coming to self-consciousness" of the Reason that is the fundamental pattern of the history of human culture or *Geist*. So the teaching of philosophy in England and in America was for half a century vitally concerned with the history of philosophy, conceived as the development of the Hegelian form of philosophical "idealism." In France, where a similar reaction against

* Bertrand Russell, *Wisdom of the West* (Garden City, N.Y.: Doubleday, 1959), pp. 5, 310.

the historical emphasis has prevailed since World War II, philosophy was taken rather as the development of the scheme of intelligibility that is science, in the teachings of men like Brunschvicg, Meyerson, and Koyré.

Now Hegel was clearly wrong in construing the history of philosophy as a unilinear development; our examination of the plurality of historical patterns it actually displays must make that clear. He was also wrong in taking that central pattern as "dialectical," that is, as generated by the "movement" of logical categories—though his original pattern of cultural history in the *Jugendschriften* is more plausible. And he showed a *hybris* impossible in our more modest days in thinking the goal of the whole process was his own *absolutes Wissen*—though again it is clear that any history is always understood as coming to a focus on our problems.

But Hegel was right in regarding philosophical thinking as cumulative. It builds up a funded body of intellectual materials and instruments, of concepts, methods, and distinctions worked out in philosophical experience. If we are aware of that cumulative process, when we use them today we use them with a sense gained of their intellectual power, of what they can do, and also of their intellectual limitations and dangers, where experience has shown they are likely to lead our thinking astray unless we be on our guard. Plato means to us the power of the idea of intelligible form, and also the danger of separating that form from its subject-matter. Aristotle means the power of the analysis of language, of taking care how things can be best said; and he means also the danger of using language to define beforehand the structure of subject-matter, instead of to express the structure we discover by consulting nature. He means also the power of a functional analysis of the processes of art and of nature, an analysis of them as the achievement of outcomes through the exercise of capacities under specific conditions. And he means also the danger of conceiving those processes in too rigid a fashion. Spinoza means the power of the idea of a unified intelligible structure, of a world that is through and through transparent to mind; and also the danger of the consequences of neglecting such important features of the experienced world as contingency, potentiality, and novelty. Hume means for us the ultimate outcome of Newtonian disconnectedness, and of taking knowledge as passive, and as verified by its origins; he means also the necessity of a manipulative and experimental conception of knowing.

This cumulative aspect of our funded body of philosophical ideas is revealed in the clarification through their use of methods, of intellectual procedures, of standards of validity. Through long experience we have found out how such methods and tests operate in practice, the consequences they entail, the difficulties they generate. We have learned the dangers of the appeal to intuition and self-evidence, especially for intellectual men too familiar with accepted ideas. We have the long criticism, both from without and from within a tradition, of the methods of rationalism, of empiricism and positivism, of the critical philosophy, and of the Hegelian dialectic. We have discovered the impasses to which each of these methods can lead, the points at which each needs an inevitable supplementing. We are familiar with the methods of the sciences, ever-developing and ever in process of being refined; we have found out why where they have succeeded they have been so successful, and something of what it is difficult or impossible for them to do. We have suffered from the intellectual consequences of confused and ambiguous ideas, with no single ascertainable meaning. We have been driven to formulate careful methods for achieving precision in clarifying ideas, and in the use of language to express them. For in philosophy, as in one of his sage *obiter dicta* Bradley remarked, we not only try to say just what we mean, but we are forever condemned to mean what we say.

Then, too, our accumulated store of philosophic wisdom includes the classic philosophic analyses. It contains the analyses of historical and familiar arguments, still appealed to today, which time has shown will not hold water. It sums up the analyses of plausible assumptions that still seduce the unwary. In it are to be found definitive analyses of problems, like Hume's examination of miracles; or the treatments given by Augustine, by Spinoza, and by Kant of the so-called problem of the freedom of the will, which must be taken into consideration by any responsible present-day fresh attempt to deal with that confused issue.

Here too belong the refinement and reformulation of philosophical concepts. Here belong the histories of the great metaphysical distinctions, elaborated and made more precise through repeated use, polished and sharpened as instruments of criticism: the one and the many, permanence and change, the real and the ideal, form and matter, potentiality and actuality, reason and experience, structure and function, and the rest. Here belong concepts like truth, meaning, value, cause, idea, happiness. All such ideas are the more manipulable, the more subject to conscious control, the more suited to serve us as intellectual instruments, as we are aware of the long critical discussion and the historical uses to which they have been subjected.

Nor can we forget the store of classic visions, of imaginative perspectives upon the world, in the light of different intellectual interests. Here is not the practice so much as the poetry of ideas. Those visions are perspectives, from differing standpoints in the activities of men and their ideal enterprises, on the same permanences of man's experience of the world. In seeking the universal structure of that world and of man's varied experience of it and in it, it is an imaginative liberation to look through as many different eyes as we may. Especially in a time when the temptation of the philosopher is to rest in his enthusiasm for his narrow and fierce technicalities, it is of vital importance to share as many visions of God as may be given to our capacities. Only thus can we hope to escape the tyranny of the one-sided and selected insistences and intellectual pressures of the present.

The major philosophers have been quite aware that no original mind can afford to cut the ties that link him with the great thinkers of his past. Each such towering figure has felt the compulsion to come to terms with his "predecessors." Even Bertrand Russell, whom Alan Wood calls ill-educated, has had to do it twice. Plato is keenly aware of the wealth of fertile ideas he has inherited from the early Greeks, and introduces them freely in his own fresh discussions. Indeed, we know about those predecessors largely because he and Aristotle found their ideas worth taking seriously. They are still enormously suggestive, so that a Heidegger can in our own day build his own sophisticated thought upon them. Aristotle's concern with his predecessors is notorious: he has a strong sense of the continuity of intellectual inquiry, and the first book of any of his writings is normally a kind of Platonic dialogue in which he argues with the "ancients."

Kant could not achieve his own critical philosophy until he had come to terms with the diverse interpretations of Newtonian thought in the eighteenth-century world. That fact makes his the classic analysis of the Newtonian assumptions, and the philosophy of science on which the nineteenth century built, when an expanded and reconstructed science made further building necessary. Hegel was keenly aware of the whole tradition, and in his imposing synthesis consciously tried to take account of all the insights of the past. He attempted to put together both Platonism and Aristotelianism. He was the first to reestablish living contact with Greek thought, after the temporary rupture in the seventeenth century. He also tried to face the problem of his own day, by combining the whole metaphysical tradition with the many eager Romantic explorations of human experience.

What is it that such thinkers go to their predecessors to learn? They go for hypotheses and suggestions, for insights that promise fruitful elaboration. They do not, to be sure, prize highly historical accuracy. From Aristotle on, the historical scholar has been able to convict them of distortion and misunderstanding—though doubts begin to arise when we moderns start proving that we can understand the early Greeks far better than Plato and Aristotle, who were at least in a position to read what they wrote. In our own day, Whitehead had a genius for finding in earlier thinkers ideas no one had ever before suspected were hidden there.

Philosophers go also to their past for points of reference, for the classic expositions of positions on which they wish to build, or against which they wish to set off their own thinking. Those who have pushed a standpoint to the limit serve an especially useful purpose. That is why the extreme positions usually receive the strongest emphasis, and give the impression that philosophical history has been a *giganto-machia*, a battle of Titans, rather than a cooperative enterprise.

They go too for the record of intellectual experiments, to find out where certain methods and assumptions have led, the consequences they have generated and the impasses they have confronted. Such sustained philosophical experimenting, conducted over several generations as the assumptions of a tradition have been worked out and pushed, is indeed the only way of criticizing those basic starting points for which we find no prior principles or *archai* from which to judge them. We have found the impasses to which a purely mechanical conception of experience has again and again led able minds. We have repeatedly seen the consequences of taking mind as purely passive in knowing. We have disconfirmed the hypothesis that the origin of ideas is a satisfactory test of their validity. Such assumptions are ultimately best criticized through their history, by a knowledge of where those hypotheses have led the inquiring mind.

Thinkers go to the past, again, to liberate themselves from the provinciality of their own tradition. The Greeks, we say, were happy in having a diversity of traditions on which to draw. In contrast, in twentieth-century Cambridge, the exigencies of the curriculum still make philosophy begin with Descartes: it is impossible to combine the classical with the philosophical tripos. American philosophizing has been fortunate in its freedom from this limitation to a single national tradition: the insularism of the British, the provinciality of the French, the self-containedness of the German. American philosophy, come of age by the end of the nineteenth century, could draw on all the different European traditions. That has something to do with the fact that the giants of the last generation could bend them all to the illumination of American experience, in creating a distinctively new and American philosophical attitude and approach.

Since the eighteenth century all our philosophies have been philosophies of experience: they have been forged as critical instruments with which to reconstruct the intellectual past. But to use a critical instrument, to understand it and to be able to handle it, it is necessary to know what it was devised to criticize. These philosophies of experience of the last two centuries have all presupposed the classic tradition coming down from the Greeks, as the subject-matter they have been enlarging. If their function and meaning is to be properly appraised, they obviously demand a knowledge of that classic tradition. We must study the classic tradition, and come to feel its intellectual power, even when we are anxious to go beyond it. Else we shall find ourselves denying what it saw, instead of placing those insights in our broader context. To go beyond is to see more, not to see less. To embrace a philosophy of criticism with no inkling of what it is criticizing, is to run the danger of the myopia into which these latter days some of us have been tempted to fall. It was some time ago pointed out that there is a great difference between studying John Dewey's philosophy of criticism alone, and studying Dewey and also what Dewey had studied and was criticizing. Many another name can be substituted for Dewey's: Nietzsche's, or Ayer's, or Wittgenstein's, or Sartre's, for instance. Dewey himself always insisted that for him the classic tradition was basic: he was taking its achievements for granted, not averting his eyes. His writings, indeed, normally start with the muddles and confusions of modern philosophy—even as those of the analysts of language—and then turn to the Greeks for a steadying direction, before going on to loosen their rigidity and set their thought in a broader context drawn from the philosophies of experience. Aristotle's thought was developed in part as a philosophy of experience to criticize the Platonists; there is a meaningful sense in which Dewey is traveling still farther on Aristotle's road. Or consider how effectively Whitehead also turned to the Greeks to find an instrument for criticizing what he called the "disconnectedness" of the Newtonian thought of the early scientific age. But such an enterprise demands knowledge of the Greeks, of the classic tradition, of the Newtonian body of ideas, and of our new concepts and techniques. Neglect of any one of these leads to philosophizing that is thin and ultimately empty.

How are we to understand our own philosophic situation and our intellectual problems today? For help in answering this vital question, we can ask, how, then, do we understand any philosophy? Well, one important answer runs, we can understand the philosophy of a great thinker genetically, that is, historically. We try to ascertain the problems he was facing, what Cassirer, a consummate master at the understanding of past philosophies, called his *Aufgabe*, his task. We try to understand the resources at his disposal, the intellectual materials available to him, the philosophical ideas and assumptions with which he can set about his task. We try to understand the limits to what he can do, the presence of recalcitrant assumptions that lend themselves only with great difficulty to his purposes—assumptions included in the tradition to which he appeals, along with the other assumptions to which he can more easily resort. We attempt to assay the toughness of the recalcitrant assumptions, how far they can be rebent and remolded.

Descartes's task was to understand and generalize his new mathematical physics in terms of the Augustinian philosophy of science. He encountered the limitations of his geometrical method when he tried to extend his ideas to the human soul itself, and was led into the impasse of the Cartesian dualism from which only Darwin was able finally to extricate Western thought. Leibniz's task was to give a mathematical formulation to the Aristotelian world of natural processes, and to make mechanics intelligible in Aristotelian terms. He encountered the fact that he had no way of accounting for the brute contingency that facts oppose to a strictly mathematical philosophy, and could never distinguish between his own inspired solutions and his brilliant but more fantastic speculations.

Kant was working within the Wolffian metaphysical version of the Leibnizian world, criticizing it from the standpoint of the German analytical empiricism and of the philosophic defense thrown up by the German Newtonian physicists, whose thought he had come to share—Rüdiger, Lambert, Euler, and the rest. He was trying to put Leibniz and Newton together, on the basis of a version of John Locke. When Kant came, in his first critique, to analyze the assumptions of Newtonian science, he found his thought succumbing at the outset to Locke, whose assumptions were at the crucial moment reinforced by Kant's reading of Tetens. So what started out in Kant as a logical analysis of Newton, was distorted by his inadequate psychology into what seemed to be a psychological analysis. In the *Analytic* Kant succeeded in working his way pretty clear of Locke and psychology, but in the *Inaugural Dissertation* and in the *Aesthetic* he is still caught in Locke's assumptions, and so like Hume presents a fusion of psychology with logic.

In his ethics, Kant is trying to put together the Enlightenment morality of the freedom of reason to follow rational law, with Newtonian determinism. Rousseau showed him how to convert rational determinism into a rational autonomy, but could not illuminate the final reconciliation between a rational freedom and a rational determinism. Kant's "timeless choice" proved the ultimate stumbling-block. In his aesthetics, Kant's *Aufgabe* was to combine Newton with the current of Romantic creative art. Here creativity won out, and made Newtonian science itself the supreme artistic creation.

Or take Whitehead, in our day a supreme statesman of ideas, a synthesizer, and not like so many of his contemporaries primarily a critic. Whitehead's thinking displays so many diverse strains, so many novel devices for bridging the gaps between them, that his philosophy can be understood only through the history of the genetic development of his thought. We have to follow the successive intellectual problems he faced, to grasp the various resources to which he turned, the limits they set to what he could do with their ideas, the tensions they developed when brought together, the concepts by means of which his mathematical imagination attempted to relieve those tensions. We approach Whitehead best through examining what he was successively trying to do, the means he found for doing it, and how he worked out the problems they generated. It is no chance that those who have understood Whitehead most easily are those who have not come upon his Gifford lectures cold, as it were, but who had followed his successive philosophical analyses from his *Principles of Natural Knowledge* and *Concept of Nature* on.

Equally, Whitehead's achievement is to be evaluated, not in terms of a quite alien program, like Russell's or Wittgenstein's, but only in terms of his own aims and problems, and his success in facing and meeting them. We can appraise the adequacy of his materials for his purposes, the degree to which the essentially structural and mechanical concepts of the assumptions of British empiricism lent themselves to the formulation of a functional philosophy of processes—the limits they set, the blind spots they induced. And such an historical and

genetic analysis makes possible a comparison in detail of the
diverse elements in Whitehead's thought. It facilitates a comparison of his problems with our own, if we are not mathematical physicists; of his materials with ours, if we are not so
committed to the British tradition; of his mathematical methods as appropriate to our problems, if we are not *animae
naturaliter Leibnizianae*. We can then adopt some of Whitehead's critical and speculative ideas, and bend them to our
own purposes and ends.

The understanding of every significant philosopher is ultimately the understanding of the materials he offers for our
own disposal, of the concepts and distinctions and methods
he has made available for use on our own problems. The
understanding of our own philosophizing—of our problems
and our intellectual resources, our philosophical situation and
the *Aufgabe* it imposes—is in the last analysis essentially the
same. Our problems too are clarified for us by a genetic and
historical analysis, which will reveal how they developed from
broad cultural conflicts, how they came to be focused more
sharply on specific issues. I choose three as illustrative.

First, we are confronted by the cultural problem of the
presence of many religions in the one world in which we are
all more closely united than ever before. These religions present us with many conflicting beliefs, a fact which focuses our
broader problem of understanding and meeting the situation
of religious pluralism on the more specific problem of the
nature of religious knowledge. Here we find a long historical
background, the emergence since the days of the Greeks of
successive schemes of understanding religious knowledge,
in the context of the problem of understanding the fact of
knowledge in philosophy and in the sciences. Our tradition

has exhibited a long wrestling with this problem, which has been confronted in many forms. The wrestling has given us concepts and distinctions that have been clarified by a long philosophical history. These are our resources. Perhaps the most promising are the great philosophical reinterpretations of the nature of religion and of religious knowledge stemming from the post-Kantian era, when it was realized and accepted that religious knowledge could not be taken as "literal," as just like scientific knowledge of the world and of man. Then come the most promising ideas. And we begin to elaborate our present understanding of religious ideas and of religious language as not literal but "symbolic." This sends us to the examination of religious and linguistic symbols, in which we are at present engaged. It takes us to the assistance offered by Hegel and Schelling, by Freud and Jung, by Cassirer and Tillich. It gives promise of helping us to understand how all these religions can express the realities of human experience, how all of them can be alike exploring the religious dimension of the world and of man's life in it, and yet speak in such diverse accents.

Second, we are confronted by the insistent cultural problem of the many diverse schemes of values exhibited in the panorama of human cultures that the anthropologist has revealed to us. This is the problem of "cultural relativity," so basic for any present-day reflection upon ethics. How can we understand this diversity of ultimate loyalties? How can we attain practical and intellectual cooperation between these different value systems? How can we build up standards of criticism, by which these conflicting goods might be made to converge? This problem too has had a long history, ever since the days when traveling Greek Sophists first turned to *physis*, or nature, to judge the many different *nomoi* they encountered in their wanderings. In that history figures centrally the Western idea of the "law of nature," often discredited but equally often resurrected in a new form. How can such a universal standard be reconstructed, to cleanse it of its obvious Western limitations? How can we feel the obligation of our own ultimate loyalties, when it has become clear they are not really ultimate, but only the best we have so far found? Here is a central problem of ethical philosophizing, for which history clearly provides a necessary illumination.

Third, there is the problem of human freedom, both practical and theoretical. How can we struggle to increase practical freedom in our world, if man is not ultimately in some sense "free"? And how are we to understand this sense? Traditionally, the problem involved the conflict between human freedom and God's foreordination and providence. Then it became the clash with the causal assumption of Newtonian science, as revealed in the analyses of Hume and Kant. Then appeared a new factor, the conception of causality implied in more recent quantum mechanics. All these conflicts demand historical analysis for their clarification. The problem comes to its sharpest focus when we ask, how are we to understand the necessary conditions of human freedom in the light of the assumptions of our science, and especially of our reigning psychologies, in which even the freedom of reason, the classic conception of human freedom, so often seems to be submerged in the unconscious, or in reflexes and sensory-motor arcs?

The intellectual resources for dealing with a fresh philosophical problem are inevitably inherited from the past. But only too often, not only the resources and materials for dealing with it, but also the problem itself, is inherited and not generated by living tensions. Thus Russell early invented a powerful new logical technique. But the problems that concerned him were the same old problems generated by the traditional assumptions of Locke. And it has been a lifelong struggle, a struggle that has never attained complete success, to try to emancipate himself from the hold of those outgrown and inherited problems. G. E. Moore was even worse off, for he has confessed he would never have been led to philosophize at all, had it not been for the curious ideas other philosophers had been able to think up. That is, he has always accepted the problems of the other man, contenting himself with offering his own careful solutions.

It has recently been claimed that the sole function of philosophy is to clear up the muddles arrived at by past philosophers, by means of the careful analysis of the misuse of language that generated them. But a far more convincing method of clearing up past muddles is historical analysis, which can so easily reveal the inconsistent and unfruitful assumptions that originally provoked them. This is the liberating and emancipating function of historical knowledge, which can so well handle the central problems of just those in the present day who most scorn the historical approach to philosophizing. Such historical and genetic analysis can eliminate problems that have become, as we say, "academic," because they are merely taken over from the past, dealing with issues that have grown unreal because they have ceased to be at the focal point of living intellectual tensions. It can eliminate the antiquated problems, because it can reveal the inconsistent assumptions that led men into them, assumptions made only because men then accepted certain ideas that are now long since abandoned.

Thus, the historical understanding of why the fact of knowledge, the very existence of the obviously going concern that was the scientific enterprise, became in the seventeenth and eighteenth centuries a central "epistemological" problem, can free us from finding it a "problem" today, when we no longer hold the purely mechanical view of the world and hence of human experience that created that dialectical "problem," under the conditions of the limited ideas about both then prevailing.

Historical knowledge and analysis can also unify the problem of the different philosophical traditions and movements which in the present are seemingly so unrelated. It can do so by tracing them all back to the common issues and factors from which they all took their origin. Thus we have noted how our critical philosophies of experience have ever since the eighteenth century, when they largely took their present form, seemed strikingly divergent, never more so than at the present day. It has often of late been remarked that communication between the different philosophical currents of our own time seems to have broken down almost completely. The American philosophies of experience, of James, Dewey, and Whitehead; the Continental phenomenological and existential philosophies, from Husserl to Heidegger and Jaspers; the logical empiricism of the Vienna Circle, of Carnap and Ayer and their followers; the linguistic analysis of the disciples of Wittgenstein at Oxford—in the present, these schools can only debate each other's very conception of the function of philosophy itself, or else cease completely from talking to each other at all. One has only to open a philosophical journal, or, still better, to attend a supposedly "international" philosophical congress, to find the Germans in one corner, the English in another, the French at one side, and the Americans vainly trying to talk to them all.

But these completely divergent—or rather, parallel currents, for they often seem never to have met at all—when viewed in historical perspective, begin to appear as all sharing a common function. They are all methods of criticizing the "abstractions" of practical common sense, or our formalized and systematized scientific schemes, by calling attention more adequately and emphatically to the generic traits of, and the distinctions forced upon men by, the world as directly encountered—by the world "immediately experienced," say the Americans; by the experienced world "phenomenologically described," say the Continentals; by the world formulated in "protocol sentences," say the logical empiricists; by the world implied in the many ways we use "ordinary language," say the elucidators of the "logical characteristics" of our manifold uses of talking. When we get below the surface differences in terminology, these very different philosophies begin to appear as the different strands in a common critical enterprise. In these many diverse forms, this enterprise is trying to rectify the inadequacies and limitations of our highly selective schemes of understanding, of our inherited intellectual assumptions, of our narrow and rigid linguistic categories, whose conflicts have generated so many purely dialectical problems and dilemmas. They rectify them by pointing to the traits and aspects of the world experienced in man's rich and varied human activities, but neglected and obscured in his various one-sided linguistic and mathematical formulations.

Each of these critical philosophies of experience has, of course, its own emphasis and its own peculiar problems. But even when these are seen and dealt with piecemeal and in detail, they are seen and treated differently when they are all viewed as the ramifications of a larger unified problem. It is the history of the last two centuries that, when understood, forces that unification upon us. And it offers the promise of a tendency toward convergence, perhaps even of an ultimate translatability from one philosophical language into the others. At least it gives hope of an eventual fruitful dialogue, of a genuine process of philosophical communication, in place of the present mutual incomprehensibility and total lack of any meeting of philosophical minds. Historical knowledge and analysis can alone hope to pierce these linguistic curtains between philosophies today.

In his last public appearance before the students at Columbia University, John Dewey gave it as his parting message, that the most important question in philosophy today is, What is philosophy itself? What is the nature and function of the philosophical enterprise? And he went on with a warning, that in a world presenting so many insistent demands for philosophical analysis, clarification, and criticism, as ours today, philosophy seems to be running the great danger, that it may become a new scholasticism, and content itself with mulling over technical trivialities and the outgrown problems inherited from past philosophers, offering no intellectual clarification and guidance to the many cultural enterprises of a confused generation.

It is indeed true, that the chief contribution history can bring to philosophic understanding, is the light it can shed on the character of philosophy itself, as men have carried it on in the tradition of our Western culture since the days of the Greeks. For history reminds us, of what when we look about us today we are sometimes tempted to forget, of the central and indispensable function philosophy has been able to perform in the long intellectual life of Western society. In the light of this long history, we can safely say:

1. Philosophy is *not* a narrow technical specialty, appealing only to a select few, with no relevance outside their limited circle, lingering on at the periphery of the central streams of our intellectual life.

2. Philosophy is *not* the concern with a small group of inherited puzzles and dilemmas, insoluble because of the contradictory character of the assumptions that create them, assumptions whose plausibility is lost in the dim past of antiquated and abandoned ideas.

3. Philosophy is *not* a collection of mistakes due to the confused misuse of language, to be cleared up by a proper analysis once and for all and then happily forgotten.

4. Philosophy *is* a clarification and criticism of the fundamental beliefs involved in all the great enterprises of human culture, science, art, religion, the moral life, social and political activity. It is especially the clarification and criticism of those beliefs that have come into conflict, normally through the impingement of fresh discovery of knowledge and novel social experience, upon inherited knowledge and wisdom.

5. Philosophy *is*, in its imaginative and poetic as distinguished from its critical function, the imaginative discernment and elaboration of new ideas, drawn from some special area; in modern times, usually from one of the sciences, but often from practical life or from religion as well; and the imaginative generalization of that fruitful idea into other areas of intellectual life.

Such a conception of the nature of the philosophical enterprise, grounded in a careful and accurate knowledge of its two millennia and a half of history in Greece and the West, since the Greeks first invented science and philosophy, a pair of twins brought forth at a single birth, can welcome what new illumination we can achieve as to the most fruitful methods and the specific aims of philosophizing today, as additional strands in a continuing function; not as the denial of everything that philosophy has been and all it has done throughout its long history. If some professional philosophers freely and with full knowledge choose to renounce this historical function, other reflective minds will arise to perform it. They will become our significant philosophers. For that function is too deeply embedded in the core of the Western intellectual tradition for our culture ever to abandon it.

Index